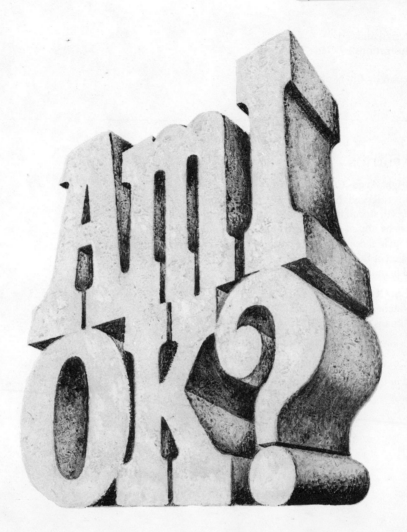

Paul L. Phillips, Ed. D.

Franklin D. Cordell, Ph. D.

Cover design and
Book illustrations by Gene Tarpey

Book design by Bill Nichol

ARGUS COMMUNICATIONS
7440 Natchez Avenue
Niles, Illinois 60648

International Standard Book Number 0-913592-57-9

Library of Congress Number 75-18895

Printed in the United States of America.

CONTENTS

chapter title and number   page

BECOMING **OK** IS EVERYONE'S POTENTIAL   **1**   4

TRANSACTIONAL ANALYSIS—A FRAME OF REFERENCE   **2**   16

NEEDS, DECISIONS, AND STROKES   **3**   28

TIME STRUCTURING   **4**   40

THE FEELING ADULT   **5**   60

GAMES ARE WAYS OF RELATING   **6**   68

FROM RESCUING TO FACILITATING   **7**   82

FROM PERSECUTING TO NEGOTIATING   **8**   94

FROM ISOLATING TO INITIATING   **9**   100

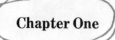 **Chapter One**

Becoming OK

At one time or another every person who wants to be happier and healthier asks, "Am I OK?" It may be the most important question you ever ask, because it can be your springboard, your motivating force, toward becoming a more OK person. "Am I OK?" can be the beginning of your social and psychological growth, and it can be the start of a happier and healthier life for you.

When you are OK, you are aware of yourself as both being and becoming. As being, you feel confident, live fully, and enjoy the present. As becoming, you are developing, building, and changing. There is no doubt that your psychological growth is as real and as important as your physical growth. But we should recognize that psychological growth is somewhat different. When it takes place unconsciously it is apt to be haphazard. It is our belief that to make truly dramatic strides in your psychological growth, you must consciously seek to grow. You must set out to achieve growth. When you actively and consciously seek growth, you are involved in the double process of being and becoming. You are being-becoming. Being-becoming is living happily in the present with confidence, and at the same time growing for the future.

Throughout this chapter and throughout the rest of this volume, you will come across words like behaving,

is everyone's potential

feeling, and doing. We use these words to indicate *now*—the present; not to indicate having behaved, having felt, or having done—the past; nor to indicate will behave, will feel, or will do—the future. Growing is a process in the present. It is *now*.

Being OK and becoming OK mean that your feelings and actions fit together. You feel more confident and can be a truly open, accepting person. You feel more secure and you can take risks with your feelings. You feel more fully social and accept and enjoy others in an authentic, nonmanipulative way. Confidence and security give you a sense of vitality and spontaneity, and creativity naturally follows. You can respond effectively to the needs of others and at the same time satisfy yourself. You can manage conflict in healthy and productive ways. You can turn games into friendly relationships.

We believe that when you are an OK person, you recognize your acting, receiving, and responding with others as a crucial part of being-becoming. You also recognize that others draw from that same interplay for their psychological growth. The interchange between the OK person and others provides the food for growth in OK-ness. You need others; they need you. You need to relate because in that dynamic interplay you achieve your psychological growth and the joy of being OK.

An ever-changing picture of what you can become is a prime goal when you are a being-becoming person. You look at your potential, your capacities, and your talents in a new, much less limited, way. You change from wanting to be somebody else to understanding and becoming the person you want to be. Living up to your potentials and developing your talents and capacities are the avenues you consciously travel—not blindly follow—as you grow and as you achieve.

When you are an OK person you are continually in process—moving, developing, changing, and becoming. When you are an OK person your vision of what you can be is moving, changing, and developing. Your changing vision of what you can be gives you a goal, a direction to your psychological growth.

Tools for Growing

You, like everyone else, have the potential to become a more joyful and social person. It takes some tools to make this happen. When you learn to use these tools, you become more aware of yourself and more aware of others. As you become more aware, you build more effective ways of living and responding to others. Listening, accepting, choosing, trusting, and opening up are all tools for growing. As you read "Am I OK?" you will learn to use these tools.

Listening to and Accepting Yourself and Others

When you are a being-becoming person, you listen to yourself and others in a special way. You listen for the things that often slip by unnoticed. You listen to and accept your feelings. You deal with those feelings in a conscious way. You listen to your body tell you how tired it is after a long day's work. When you listen to yourself for the first time, you will become conscious that you are embarrassed, fearful, disappointed, angry, or confident. Being conscious of your feelings helps you accept them as natural. Other people in the same situation feel the same way. Your feelings are OK even when the situation that caused them is not. When you listen to and accept your feelings you are in the driver's seat, selecting your own avenues of growth.

Listening tells you what you think you can and cannot do. It tells you what you want and do not want, or maybe it tells you that you are confused about what you want. Listening is knowing yourself—knowing about yourself. It tells you when you are confused, what you feel, what you think you should or should not do, that you are hurt, embarrassed, happy, or tired.

 When discussing his feelings, Bill M. said that he felt depressed and that he did not know why. "I feel frustrated because I don't know where these feelings come from. Everything was going along okay, then, all of a sudden, I started to feel depressed." After learning to listen to himself, Bill recognized the source of his feelings and described them as feelings of rejection, anger, and disappointment at not getting a promotion a few weeks earlier.

When Bill listened to himself, he learned that he was not simply angry or disappointed but, most of all, feeling rejected. Not being promoted was a blow to his pride. When he finally listened to his feelings of rejection, he also understood that they were the starting point of the anger and disappointment and, finally, his feelings of depression.

Listening made Bill's feelings clear. Accepting them

helped him deal effectively with his feelings and with the people who were part of those feelings. For Bill, describing his feelings let others know what he felt, and that in itself made his feelings easier to deal with.

When you listen in that special way to others, you begin to see that sometimes even grown-ups have a child inside —playing, teasing, or reaching out for love and understanding. Often that child reaches out in negative ways —by demanding, grasping, or sulking. The child inside covers its fears with a tough-guy mask, its confusion with a mocking sureness. Sometimes the child covers its loneliness with defiance and its hurt with anger. When you listen, you hear that child reaching out. Then you can do what makes both the grown-up and the child inside you happy.

Sometimes when you listen in that special way, you hear a parent inside, worried that some danger threatens the people he or she loves. Sometimes that parent shows concern by being bossy, by giving orders, or by taking over. Knowing that parent helps you respond in a positive way.

As does everyone else, you have a basic set of impulses, hungers, feelings, and strivings. Part of becoming a grown-up human being is learning to deal with those basics in productive ways. As did everyone else, however, you probably learned how to deal with those impulses and hungers when you were a child. Some of the ways you learned were mindless, troublesome, and destructive. You learned to strike out, to withdraw, or to sulk. You may have learned to simply reject those feelings and impulses —to push them aside—only to learn later that some of them are so strong that they come back in new ways. For

instance, everyone needs rest after working hard. Take
this example:

> Mary S. worked ten hours a day and more. When
> she got home at night she would work some more.
> She was tired, worn out; but she could not accept
> the feelings of tiredness because she had learned
> early in her life that "good people work hard—
> they work hard all the time." This was important,
> because when Mary rested she felt guilty. She was
> nagged by the feeling that she should be doing
> more. This robbed her of the time needed to refresh
> herself, to regenerate her spirit, to be a growing
> person. When Mary learned to listen to herself and
> to accept her feelings, she recognized that her
> guilt was a carry-over from her childhood. She
> eventually learned to overcome her guilt and, as
> the fairy tales say, "lived happily ever after."

How do you learn to listen to self and others? First,
you learn about feelings, needs, and your relationships
with other people. Then you study the people and things
that formed you into the person you are. You study the
experiences of your childhood and your present-day experiences. You come to understand that each of us has a
Child and a Parent we carry around with us. Finally, you
study your relationships with other people. That is what
this book is about.

Trusting Self and Others
Trusting, as something you consciously plan, is managing
or setting aside your fears and treating yourself and
others as though you expect the best of them. Trusting

is not just "whistling a happy tune," because trusting does not deny fear but consciously sets it aside. Trusting is sending the message: "I'm real; I'm predictable; I won't reject you; I won't switch roles and persecute you."

Carlos was afraid that his friends would reject him. He could not trust them to accept him as he was. So Carlos thought that he had to do just what others asked of him. He was manipulated by others. His life was not his own. He lived just to meet other people's expectations. He was afraid to assert himself because he thought that if he did he would lose friendships. In defense, Carlos himself became manipulative. To gain control of his life, Carlos had to set aside his fear of rejection and trust someone, at least for a while.

Cindy was afraid to trust her feelings about her own abilities as a student. She could not trust her feelings of success, and she could not trust the teacher's reassurance. She felt that if she was not always successful, the teacher and others would reject her. Things became so bad that Cindy would not risk giving answers in class for fear of being wrong. She would write her assignments but not turn them in because she was afraid she would be rejected and criticized if they were wrong.

Both Carlos and Cindy had so little confidence in themselves that they could not trust others. Their lack of confidence magnified their fear of rejection. What both of them needed most was to receive the trust and support of others. But trust works two ways. You sometimes have to trust others before others can trust you. Trust builds confidence in both parties. Suspicion builds walls between people and fosters fear and animosity.

Trusting means you seek the goal of positive friendly relationships rather than the appearances of being "cool," tough, or bright. In his book *Love Is Not Enough*, Bruno

Bettelheim shows just how crucial trust is in rebuilding the lives of emotionally disturbed children. When you trust others, you send the message: "I will not hurt you; I will not switch roles and persecute you." Bettelheim's children responded to that message by learning to trust in return.

Trusting yourself gives you the power to make decisions; it also gives you a certain toughness to help you survive setbacks. You become able to make decisions because you do not need to maintain the image of being without flaw. You trust that other people will accept you when you make mistakes.

Trusting is like making a positive prediction about yourself, and, because you make it, it comes true. When you trust others, they "hear" you become trustworthy.

People learn to not trust early in life—as soon as they are old enough to play psychological games. Games cause people to be suspicious, fearful, insecure, and vindictive. To become a more trusting person, you learn to transform psychological games into close friendships. To become more trusting, you take risks with your feelings. You learn to deal with your own not-OK feelings. You learn that you are OK. You learn to predict how people will respond, and you learn to listen to people's feelings—to accept them and to respond to them. You learn to tell people that they are OK.

Choosing OK-ness
Choosing OK-ness is the process of being aware of possibilities in your life, of understanding the consequences of selecting one possibility, and, finally, of selecting one. Choosing is recognizing that you can make things happen

in your own life. It means recognizing the outcomes of your own actions and evaluating them. And it means selecting possibilities that make good things happen to yourself and others.

Choosing OK-ness is based upon a clear perception of who you are and how the world works. That is achieved by listening and accepting, and by trusting self and others. Choosing is understanding the ways you are connected with others so that you can predict the consequences of one behavior or the other. Finally, choosing is insight into your needs, worries, and fears.

Every day you have to choose. People often choose the option that helps them avoid pain or solves a problem on a short-term basis but has damaging results in the long run. Try some of these:

When you feel angry, hurt, or rejected—instead of hiding your feelings, choose to disclose them.

When you feel like blaming someone—instead of blaming, choose to examine the other person's point of view.

When you see people who make you feel uncomfortable—instead of ignoring them, choose to approach them and make them feel OK.

When you find yourself
making excuses—instead of
rejecting responsibility
for something you have said
or done, choose to
accept responsibility.

When someone "turns off"
to you—instead of just
feeling rejected, choose
to find out why it happened.

When you feel not OK—
instead of continuing
to believe negative things,
consciously choose
to change your beliefs.

Opening to Life

Opening to life is actively seeking new experiences and new ways to understand yourself and others. Opening up is based in OK-ness—the confidence and wonder of being OK.

In his book *The Open and Closed Mind,* Milton Rokeach shows that our beliefs and our personalities develop around a set of expectations formed early in life. These expectations are about self, others, and the meaning and nature of the universe. He found that people who believe and expect negative things usually see themselves as powerless. They have a high level of anxiety and tend to become authoritarian and closed-minded; they see others as dangerous, and they see the universe as threatening. Because of the anxiety, such individuals close out new experiences and people, and seek the comfort of a set of beliefs that never change and a set of friends who never challenge them. In current slang, they are "up tight." In psychological terms, they are defensive.

You become open to life by rooting out those negative expectations and replacing them with confidence, trust, and wonder at the universe.

Laughing with Self and Others

When you learn to listen to and accept yourself and others—when you trust yourself and others—you gain the confidence to be open. Openness helps us to get a fresh perspective on things we live with every day. We begin to see the funny things in our lives. For the first time the things that have been so grim in our lives come into perspective.

"Am I OK?" is the central question asked by each person consciously engaged in growing. Asking that question is, as you have learned, a springboard, a motivating force, for realizing your potential. One basic potential stands out above all else: Your life can be fresh, dynamic, spontaneous, and joyful; it can be punctuated by peak experiences and times of close, satisfying relationships. Living can be filled with joy instead of anxiety, confidence instead of fear, spontaneity instead of hesitancy, and friendship instead of loneliness. Instead of settling for a life of safety and security, you can choose a joyful life of sharing your spontaneous energy and vitality with others.

SELF JOURNAL

Purpose
The purpose of this exercise
is to establish a clearer
and more complete
self-knowledge.

Materials
A spiral notebook
and a pencil.

Method
Select some time during the day
when you have free time
to write in your Self Journal.
You will make two kinds of entries:
one describing one or more
important events during that day,
and one describing
how you felt about the event or events.
"Listen" for your primary feelings
as you record them.
Keep the journal
for two weeks.
Is there a pattern of feelings?

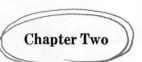

Chapter Two

Transactional

Transactional Analysis (TA) is an approach to social psychiatry developed by the late Dr. Eric Berne and popularized in several books, the most popular of which was *Games People Play*. While Transactional Analysis was developed primarily for use in psychotherapy, the authors of this book have found that psychologically healthy people can use many of its ideas to more fully understand themselves and their relationships with others, and ultimately to become happier, healthier, and more productive. Transactional Analysis helps these people understand where their feelings and behaviors originate, and provides them with guidelines for happier and healthier ways to behave.

Your Personality

The brain records each person's experiences from birth. Recordings capture the sounds, sights, textures, tastes, and feelings of everyday life. The warm glowing smile of a supporting and loving parent, the fear created by a growling dog, the bright yellow-gold flame of a match—all these and much more are a part of the experiences recorded.

Each person can recall some of the events of the past directly. Other recordings are not consciously remembered, but are important because they are *replayed* in a more fundamental and dramatic way. For instance, Sally, when criticized, gets that "sinking feeling." Sally may not consciously remember the situation in which she first experienced that reaction, but the feeling and the response are replayed.

analysis a frame of reference

Three Ego States

All of us know, without being told, that we are somehow made up of different parts. For instance, when Jim asks himself "Why did I eat those cookies when I am on a diet?" or "Why was I so mean to Mary Lou?" he experiences one part of himself talking to another part of himself. Transactional Analysis shows that Jim's personality is made up of three parts, or ego states, called the Parent, the Child, and the Adult. Each ego state is relatively separate from the others, and each has its own set of feelings, beliefs, and behavior patterns. Sometimes people act in one ego state, sometimes in another, and sometimes in two ego states at the same time.

Your Parent

The Parent ego state is a way of thinking, acting, feeling, and believing similar to that of our parents. This state develops during the first five years or so of life. Your Parent is based upon your brain's recordings of your real parents. The Parent responds immediately and automatically to childlike behavior and to various situations requiring a "take charge" response.

Your Parent:

1	2	3
establishes rules of conduct and sets limits in a commanding tone of voice.	enforces the rules by quoting them in a confident or demanding tone of voice.	teaches manners and socializes by rewarding and punishing.

17

4

supports and helps others
by reassuring
and doing things for them.

5

judges who and what are
right for self, according to
the admonitions and
regulations stored in the
memory.

6

maintains traditions
and rules of culture
by teaching, preaching,
and giving advice.

7

protects the weak, fearful,
and ignorant
by standing up for them.

8

restrains Your Child.

You can expect the Parent when you hear a command-
ing tone of voice, a warning, or a nurturing voice saying:
"You had better; You should; You must; I'm telling you;
Aw, poor little thing; Cut that out; Come sit on my lap."

Your Child

The Child ego state contains a person's basic desires and needs, and the recordings of the feelings and reactions he or she had as a child. This state develops during the same time as the Parent state. We will discuss two parts of the Child: the Natural, or Spontaneous, Child (that is, the Child as it naturally feels and acts upon its needs, desires, and impulses) and the Adapted Child (that is, the Natural Child responding to parental requests and admonitions). The spontaneous dimensions of the Child provide the joy, motivation, and natural creativity of the personality as seen in play. The adapted elements of the Child are expressed in the feelings and patterns of response to parental stimuli—responses such as rebellion, procrastination, or compliance.

Your Natural Child is:

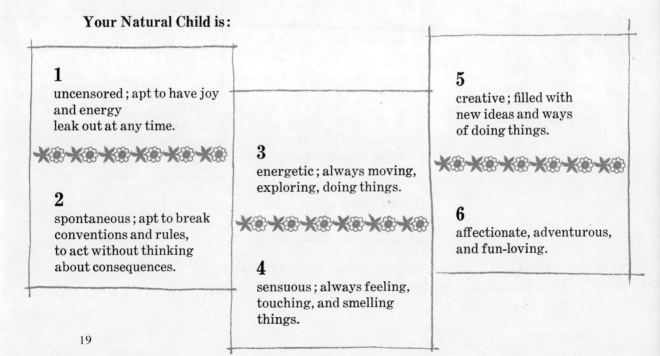

1
uncensored; apt to have joy and energy
leak out at any time.

2
spontaneous; apt to break conventions and rules, to act without thinking about consequences.

3
energetic; always moving, exploring, doing things.

4
sensuous; always feeling, touching, and smelling things.

5
creative; filled with new ideas and ways of doing things.

6
affectionate, adventurous, and fun-loving.

Your Adapted Child:

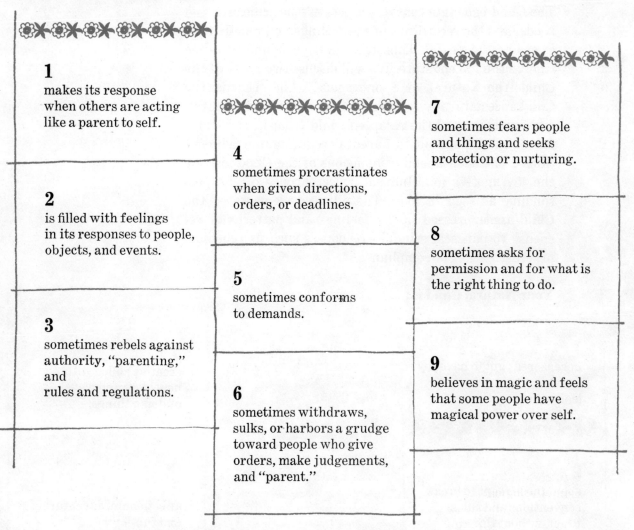

1

makes its response
when others are acting
like a parent to self.

2

is filled with feelings
in its responses to people,
objects, and events.

3

sometimes rebels against
authority, "parenting,"
and
rules and regulations.

4

sometimes procrastinates
when given directions,
orders, or deadlines.

5

sometimes conforms
to demands.

6

sometimes withdraws,
sulks, or harbors a grudge
toward people who give
orders, make judgements,
and "parent."

7

sometimes fears people
and things and seeks
protection or nurturing.

8

sometimes asks for
permission and for what is
the right thing to do.

9

believes in magic and feels
that some people have
magical power over self.

The Child uses words like: "I can't; I won't; Okay I
will; You always get to; I'll do it later; I don't want; I
want; I need; Let's go."

Your Adult

The Adult part of the personality develops later than that of the Parent and the Child. According to Berne, it starts at about ten months of age. In a healthy person the Adult continues to develop throughout life. This sets the Adult apart from the Parent and the Child. The Adult is the data processor, the scientific part of the personality. The Adult processes current and objective information about the world. The Adult does two things. First, the Adult part of the personality is responsible for most activity and work, such as driving a car, solving a problem, or learning a skill. Second, the Adult edits the recordings of the Parent and the Child when they contain inaccurate data. This is a most crucial job because it is often through the Adult that a person roots out old beliefs, feelings, and behaviors and replaces them with new, more effective ways of behaving, feeling, and reacting.

The Adult ego state is a way of acting, feeling, and believing that is objective, in the present, computing and managing new data.

Your Adult:

1
is thoughtful, using the logical processes of analysis and reflection.

2
acts in a controlled and measured way based upon consideration of the facts.

3
gathers information, sorts it, stores it, and uses it when appropriate; considers alternatives based upon the facts before deciding.

4

solves problems
in a systematic way.

5

reacts to situations
primarily in the here-and-
now rather than with
old feelings or beliefs.

6

judges after consideration
of alternatives
and consequences.

7

thinks about
different possible futures
for self and others.

8

updates beliefs
in the Parent and the Child.

9

turns off feelings of fear,
insecurity, and rejection
when they are unrealistic.

10

brings together the beliefs,
feelings, and responses
of the Parent and the Child.

11

is creative, seeking
new ways to see and
interpret things and events.

To summarize, then, the personality is made up of three relatively distinct and consistent patterns of feeling, believing, and behaving called ego states. The Parent is formed early in life and records the actual behavior of a person's parents. You are "in" the Parent ego state when you are behaving, feeling, and responding as your parents did. The Child ego state contains the uncensored and spontaneous aspects of the personality as well as the adaptations made in response to parental demands and nurturing behaviors. The Adapted Child is formed early in life in response to Parent-type behaviors.

The Adult part of the personality starts to develop at around ten months, along with the development of language and the beginnings of experience accumulation. The Adult part of the personality has two functions. It relates to the world in the here-and-now by processing current data; it also edits archaic recordings in the Parent and the Child parts of the personality.

Why study personality? One reason is that many people feel that parts of their lives are, at least at times, out of control. They have feelings and ways of reacting they would like to control. The starting point in gaining control is self-knowledge. The following exercises are provided to help you uncover problems in your Parent, Adult, and Child.

IDENTIFYING EGO STATES

Each of the following situations is accompanied by one Parent, one Adult, and one Child response. Place P, A, or C in each blank to indicate in which ego state the response originates. Because you cannot see or hear the respondent, you will have to make an educated guess. Reading all three responses before answering might be helpful.

1

The boss fills his extra-large cup with coffee and puts a dime in the kitty.

p	"You should pay twenty cents if you want to do the right thing."
c	"He thinks he's better than we are, but he's not."
a	"I wonder if he's aware that some resent his taking so much coffee for a dime?"

2

The duplicating machine breaks down.

a	"Would you call a repairman, Jane?"
p	"Nothing's the way it used to be; people just don't take pride in their work anymore."
c	"Why does this always have to happen to me?"

3

A foreman finds a workman smoking in a restricted, no-smoking area of the plant.

p	"You know its against the rules to smoke here!"
a	"Are you aware of the rule against smoking in this area?"
c	"Hey-y-y! I sure could use a drag off that cigarette."

4

A teacher's request to teach Transactional Analysis has just been refused.

c	"He wouldn't even listen to my side of the story."
a	"I think the potential benefits derived from teaching TA are well worth the problems which might arise."
p	"Anybody with any brains could see the value in teaching TA to students!"

5

Public-service employees are waiting for the departmental meeting to begin.

a	"I wonder what the nature of the meeting is?"
c	"If he (the superintendent) thinks I'm going to sit here and listen to him tell us what a great worker he is, he's nuts!"
p	"We should have an agenda before *every* meeting."

6

A student is late for class and hands the teacher a tardy slip.

p "You're late again! There must be something wrong with you."

c "I can't teach school when you students are always late."

a "Join the group in the center of the room. They will bring you up-to-date."

7

A very shapely young woman walks into the office wearing a tight jump suit.

c "Now that is outasight!"

a "What is she saying about herself by dressing in that manner?"

p "Anyone with a sense of decency wouldn't dress that way!"

8

The bulletin reminds the workers that, "You are required to stay in the building until 3:30. This means YOU!"

c "Who does he think I am, his slave?"

a "It seems Mr. Jones is disturbed about some of us leaving before 3:30."

p "It's about time the law was laid down!"

9

The faculty is discussing whether students should play chess during study hall.

p "Everyone knows study hall is for studying, not playing."

a "What effect will allowing students to play chess have on the educational atmosphere of the study hall?"

c "I really fear the wrath of the angry parents of some of the students!"

10

"You are without a doubt the worst teacher I have ever had!" says an angry student.

a "I can see you are very angry with me and expect me to teach differently."

p "I have done everything that could possibly be done for you. It's about time you grow up!"

c "I have done everything I could possibly do for you. You make me want to quit teaching."

The following answers are suggested. You might have a different answer which is reasonable and justifiable. Discussion of differences is invited.

1.	2.	3.	4.	5.	6.	7.	8.	9.	10.
P	A	P	C	A	P	C	C	P	A
C	P	A	A	C	C	A	A	A	P
A	C	C	P	P	A	P	P	C	C

KNOWING YOUR PARENT

You can become more aware of Your Parent by listening to the inflection of your voice, observing your gestures and posture, and thinking about your facial expressions.

You might even be able to remember the actions and voice inflections of your parental figures and see the similarities between yours and theirs.

In some cases you might even re-experience feelings similar to those shown by your parental figures.

Sometimes what you believe about people, money, work, leisure, and other things is very similar to your parents' beliefs about those same things.

1

List one verbal admonition you remember your parents giving you about each of the following topics :

a How children should act when speaking to adults
b How children should act in school
c How children should act at the dinner table
d How children should act to be safe from harm

2

Describe your parents' behavior when :

a you were afraid of the dark.
b you were ill.
c you failed to do your chores.
d you did not get up on time in the morning.
e you rebelled.

3

Describe what things, people, or situations trigger you into the Parent.

KNOWING YOUR CHILD

You can be aware of Your Child by listening to the tone of your voice, observing your gestures and posture, and reflecting on your facial expressions. You might be able to remember a time during childhood when you felt or believed in a manner similar to the way your parents felt and believed. Some persons might be able to reexperience the same kinds of feelings experienced during childhood.

1
Describe the feeling you had when one of your parents found out that you had violated a family rule. This was a serious rule, and your parent was angry or seriously disappointed. Do you ever have that feeling now?

2
Some children develop a style of procrastination when dealing with orders from parents. Can you remember using procrastination with your parents? In what situations did you use it? Do you still use it?

3
Many adults fear criticism by their supervisors or others. This can be tied to the "sinking feeling" Child response. Do you ever have that "sinking feeling"? In what situations do you have it?

4
Describe three times when you function in the Child.

5
Describe what things trigger you into becoming the Child.

Chapter Three

Needs, decisions,

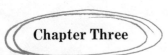

As we look at the way people conduct their lives, we are struck by the vast differences in life styles and life courses. Some people seem to live a life style, or course, determined early in life. Much like a rocket being sent to the moon, the greatest part of some life journeys is determined in advance and somehow programed into the mechanism. Other people seem to wander through life. They seem to have no specific direction or goal. They seem to be dominated at random by people and events beyond their control. Still other people seem to develop a life course similar to that of an explorer. They are involved in life; they are curious about it; they live their lives in happy and healthy ways.

Life Scripts

Transactional Analysis studies the differences in life courses through the medium of life scripts. A life script is a life plan based upon a decision made early in life, possibly when the person is only five or ten years of age. This decision is made by the Child part of the personality, and is therefore based upon distortions and inadequate information. Life scripts are experienced in three degrees of severity that range from binding, driving, *tragic scripts* to what Claude Steiner calls *banal scripts.*

Tragic scripts are those that lead to some tragic end in life, such as suicide or some other form of self-destruction. Banal scripts are those that have less dramatic proportions, but reflect our sense of identity and cause us to

and strokes

relate to other people in a way that limits our lives. Instead of becoming beautiful, loveable, and creative, we become inhibited, closed, and separated from other people.*

Current writers on Transactional Analysis present two ideas of OK-ness. The difference in these ideas is important because the difference provides a key to becoming more OK. The idea presented by Thomas Harris in his book *I'm OK, You're OK* suggests that the primary life position is I'm *not* OK, you're OK. In *Scripts People Live*, Claude Steiner takes exception to that position, proposing that each of us is OK, tough, beautiful, loveable, loving, resilient, capable, creative, exploratory, dynamic, self-correcting, and happy from birth. The negative "parenting" of our mothers and fathers and of the institutions around us erode our sense of OK-ness. The general sense of being OK or not OK takes specific form in beliefs such as, "I can do whatever I choose" or "I'm stupid." The decision is then made to live in a way that conforms to the life position. Some decisions are more binding than others throughout life, and the most binding decisions lead to third-degree scripts. Second- and first-degree life scripts are less binding. In Steiner's language, we are all born princes and princesses until we are turned into frogs by the magic spells of our parents. Remember, the Adapted Child in each person believes in magic.

In Steiner's language, the spell is cast by the commands and attributions of our parents. Commands such as "always be friendly, never say no, never show your anger, never be hostile, and don't cry" are recorded in the

*For an extensive elaboration of the forms of life scripts, read *What Do You Say After You Say Hello?* by Eric Berne and *Scripts People Live* by Claude Steiner.

Adapted Child part of our personalities. These commands limit the ways we respond to the world and thus play an important part in limiting the quality of our lives. Attributions are made when a parent, usually in the presence of others, tells who or what we are: "You're a real tough kid" or "You're a real football player" or "You're a rascal." Attributions are *like* magic to the young person who is almost defenseless against them. Attributions tell the youngster who or what he or she is, thus establishing a life course. The Child part of the personality in each individual makes a decision based upon the injunctions and attributions of the parents, and this decision defines the individual's life script.

Life scripts are sometimes supported by information contained in the Adult. The details of the life script are often based upon a child's story, a play, or a television show. The Child chooses models based on the script. The process defining the life course is, for some, complete. The power of the decision is interesting. The decision establishes a self-fulfilling prophecy which functions like magic. As soon as the individual believes that he or she is this or that kind of person, then that individual begins to relate to things and people in terms of that belief. The prophecy comes true *because* he or she believes it.

The life script is maintained through the belief itself, the support of other individuals, and the schools. In some instances the spell can be maintained simply by believing in it. Voodoo and witchcraft are probably examples of the strength of a belief in a destiny or a life course. Negative beliefs and tragic scripts are often reinforced within our institutions. We are ranked, evaluated, probed, programed, examined, and criticized constantly within our institutions. Television tells us what it is to be a beautiful person; the schools tell us what it is to be a successful person; our parents continually reinforce a particular notion of what the good person does.

Often people living by a tragic life script manipulate others through second- and third-degree games. Banal life scripts are maintained by structuring time around pastimes or rituals.

Changing the Life Script

Can a life script be changed? Can a script be set aside or bypassed? The answer is unconditionally, YES.

There are two parts, or phases, to setting aside a tragic or limiting life script—reversing the decision; and establishing a more effective and healthy life style, one that no longer supports the unwanted script.

Parents laid down the injunctions and attributions that led to the decision to opt for a certain life position. They can help change that decision. The injunctions and attributions were made out of the Child and were received in the Child. When parents are still around, an adult discussion can be very profitable.

Each individual, through the functioning in the Adult, can think his or her way through the basic decision to change a life script. A person can "lift the spell" through an analysis of the reasonableness or unreasonableness of the injunctions and attributions upon which the life script is based. A certain difficulty arises when there are injunctions against taking one's own counsel. In cases where this is true, that particular injunction must be changed before any real progress can be made.

Psychological Hungers

Each person hungers for the stimulation that comes with human interaction, for recognition from other people, and for ways to organize time to satisfy those hungers. Psychological hungers are like the hunger for food. When satisfaction is postponed, the hunger increases until the person becomes dominated by it. And if satisfaction is postponed long enough, the person will become weakened and ill. When a person lives for long stretches of time without properly satisfying psychological needs, he or she will become increasingly weakened and unhealthy. After that, when the hungers are adequately satisfied, the person becomes healthy again.

Stroking (being recognized either verbally or nonverbally) satisfies those psychological hungers. When the psychological hungers are *not* adequately satisfied—when there is too little positive stroking—feelings of confusion, abandonment, and not-OK-ness well up in the person. When that happens, the person either tries harder to satisfy the hunger by manipulating others, withdraws in confusion and frustration, or denies the need for satisfaction. Each of these strategies eventually intensifies the hungers and cuts the person off from others, building isolation and loneliness. On the other hand, when the hungers are satisfied, the person feels OK and creative energy is released. This energy can be used to become a more OK person and to help others become OK.

The secret of success, then, is to become conscious of our hungers and to structure our time to adequately satisfy them.

There are three different kinds of strokes—positive, negative, and discounting. Positive stroking is recognition

32

that stimulates and leads to positive feelings and beliefs about self and others. Positive strokes are when Geri comes home from school and says, "Hi Mom," or when the boss walks into the office and says, "Good morning, Sam, that was a great job you did in the meeting yesterday," or when an acquaintance waves from across the street.

Negative stroking stimulates a person just as positive stroking does, but it has some unwanted side effects. Negative strokes come from the judgmental Parent or from the rebellious Child. They make one feel rejected and lead to not-OK feelings and beliefs about self and others. Mom shakes her finger and says to Jimmy, "I told you never to do that!" That is a negative stroke. When people learn to accept only negative strokes, they are in a serious bind. They *need* the negative strokes to satisfy their hunger for stimulation. But in satisfying it, their needs for attention, love, and security are intensified.

Discounting strokes come from the Child masquerading as the Adult. They diminish your sense of value and worth. They "put you down." Discount stroking not only fails to build OK feelings and beliefs, but it reinforces psychologically toxic feelings and beliefs. When Jimmy says sarcastically, "Thanks, Mom," after being told to always say "thanks," that is a discounting stroke for Mom. When a wife asks her husband, "Would you like spaghetti or steak this evening?" and the husband replies, "Yes, I would," that is a discounting stroke. Being aware of discounting strokes is crucial in understanding human behavior because such strokes provoke a surge of strong not-OK feelings—a sense of abandonment, rebellion, or disgust. And that means trouble.

Getting and Giving Strokes

Stroking is vitally important to developing and maintaining feelings and beliefs that I am OK and that others are OK. The following are some problems associated with stroking patterns people learn:

1

The most basic problem is that many times people do not consciously recognize their hungers and consequently never take effective action to satisfy them. Not recognizing psychological hungers results in vague feelings of loneliness, restlessness, boredom, and irritation. Sometimes feelings become confusing and frustrating.

2

Many of the people the authors have talked with simply do not have effective ways of asking for positive strokes. Even when they are aware of their feelings, such people are incapable of asking for strokes. This situation is often reinforced by parental admonitions to not show feelings or not ask embarrassing questions, or to the command: "Get lost!"

3

Part of the process of becoming healthier and meeting our own needs is a recognition of the needs of others. A rule of thumb states that if you are to get positive strokes, you have to give them when needed. Stingy people, or people who appear to be stingy because they fail to pay attention to others, often wind up excluded.

4

Many people do not have immediate or automatic ways of giving positive strokes. Again, this pattern is reinforced by parental admonitions such as, "It's not proper to show your feelings; You must not hug other people or show approval to others."

5

Finally, many people turn down, or discount, the positive strokes others offer. For some people it is a matter of pride; for others it is a case of never having learned to feel good about being loved and accepted by others.

It seems that each of us needs to develop legitimate, healthy, productive, and "growthful" ways of satisfying those hungers in ourselves and in others. The following exercises are provided to help you listen to your needs and develop new ways to respond to them.

AWARENESS EXERCISE ONE

The purpose of this exercise is to help you listen to yourself and your needs. Put an X in either the "Yes" or "No" column.

	YES	NO
1 I often use sarcasm.		
2 People seek me out to talk to them.		
3 When I talk to people I often go away feeling hurt, rejected, or uncomfortable.		
4 I find it difficult to say positive things about other people.		
5 I am lonely much of the time.		
6 When people compliment me, I don't know what to say.		
7 I do silly things to get attention.		
8 I give discounting strokes regularly.		
9 I think some people avoid me.		
10 I feel a real sense of warmth with some people.		
11 I trust other people.		
12 I often get angry when people criticize me.		
	YES	NO

Now that you have listed your own responses, reverse your responses in your imagination. How would you respond to your friends if you were reversed? Do you like yourself better in any ways when you are reversed? Would your friends like you better if some responses were reversed?

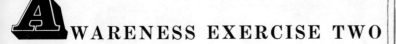

AWARENESS EXERCISE TWO

The purpose of this exercise is to raise your level of awareness of the various kinds of strokes and the ways you give them.

List the names of the last three people you talked to.

1 _____

2 _____

3 _____

Try to recall the conversation or interaction you had with each person and list the number of positive, negative, and discounting strokes you gave each person.

	positive	negative	discounting
person 1			
person 2			
person 3			

List the names of the same three people in order of their significance, closeness, or importance to you.

Did you give positive strokes to the person closest to you?

1 _____

2 _____

3 _____

Did you give any negative or discounting strokes?

36

POSITIVE STROKING

Positive strokes are warm, accepting, direct, and understanding ways of relating to others.

Often people cannot give and accept positive strokes because of parental blocking, or because they just do not have the automatic responses to give and accept them. This exercise should help you become more aware of the needs we all have for positive stroking, and should make you think of some ways to give and accept positive strokes.

This exercise is to be done with at least one other person. Introduce yourself to your partner and tell him or her one unique thing about yourself. Be attentive as you listen to your partner's comments on what you said. Respond to your partner by saying something that is warm, accepting, direct, and understanding.

1 Describe the feelings you had just prior to giving the positive stroke. Did you feel hesitant?

2 Describe your feelings when you received the positive stroke.

Many people feel that planning a stroke or asking for a stroke would appear to be inappropriate or manipulative. Yet we all need strokes. Discuss those feelings with your partner.

NEGATIVE STROKING

The purpose of this exercise is to help you become more aware of the motivations and needs that give rise to negative stroking. If negative stroking is less effective than positive stroking, why do people provoke others to give negative strokes?

1 Think of one person you know who seems to need negative strokes. Write the name here.

2 Have you ever really listened to that person? What feelings does that person have that moves him or her to seek negative strokes?

3 How does that person provoke negatives strokes?

4 What is that person's response to negative strokes?

Sometimes a person involved in negative stroking cannot accept a positive stroke. Can you give such a person a positive stroke and make it stick?

ANATOMY OF ISCOUNTING

This exercise should help you become more aware of discounting stroking patterns. You may do this exercise by yourself.

1 Try to recall the last time
you received
a discounting stroke.
Who gave it to you?

2 What led up to the discount?
What do you think you did
to provoke the discount?

3 What were your feelings
when it happened?

4 What did you say or do
when it happened?

5 Was there a hidden message
in the discount?

6 In what ego state
did you receive the discount?

7 Can you think of
an appropriate Adult
response to the discount?

STROKING JOURNAL

This exercise is intended to help you build more positive stroking patterns. It can be done alone.

1 Name a person you would like to know better and relate to in friendlier and more positive ways.

This person might be a co-worker, a neighbor, a classmate, someone you do not know at this time, or someone in your family.

Write the person's name here.

2 What do you know about this person? Have you really paid any attention to him or her? Try to list as many details as you can about the person.

3 Recall the strokes that you gave this person the last time you saw him or her. Did you give this person any positive strokes?

4 Did you give any negative strokes?

5 Did you give any discounting strokes?

6 Since you would like to know this person better and would like to have better relations with this person, write down what you think would be the most appropriate way to give this person an intense, positive stroke the next time you meet.

Think about what you like in this person. Is this person especially attractive or talented, or is he or she someone you would just like to know better?

Chapter Four

People choose to use or structure time in definite ways. Time structuring has an important impact upon who we are and who we become. Some ways of time structuring help satisfy psychological needs and ultimately help people to feel OK and to grow. Other ways of structuring time keep people in a rut of painful or unfulfilling relationships.

Six Ways To Use Time

Time structuring is sometimes done consciously and intentionally in order to satisfy hungers. Most people probably structure their time without regard for their own psychological needs or for the effect on other people. Eric Berne describes six ways of structuring time: withdrawal, rituals, pastimes, activities, games, positive friendly relationships. The first is a way of structuring time alone. The other five are ways of structuring time with other people.

Withdrawal

Withdrawal is the act of a person who consciously chooses to be apart from other people. Withdrawal seems to happen in two different ways. First, people who have worked all day, or have been with others all day, might feel stimulated sufficiently; they thus choose to withdraw, to be by themselves. It is as though the individual chooses to regroup, to calm down. Very healthy people withdraw for self-renewal, to be creative, or simply to rest. Second, people withdraw because their relationships with others are painful. They have had it! In that instance, withdrawal is a defense against a world they just cannot manage.

40

STRUCTURING

Rituals

When people ritualize, they exchange mild and highly predictable strokes. Daily greetings, introductions, and good-byes are common rituals. Rituals are very important because they provide a means of stroking without requiring much time or much involvement with other people. When the boss walks down the hall and initiates a ritual with, "Hi, Jim," the expected response is something like, "Hello, Ms. Allen!" A rule governs rituals. Most people unconsciously adhere to it. The rule is that you must give as many strokes as you get—not too many, not too few. If a person gives too many strokes, then others become suspicious. When Frank says, "Hi, Jim," he expects the response, "Good morning, Frank," or something equal to one stroke. Frank might say, "Hi, Jim," and Jim responds, "Well, hello there, Frank! How are you today? It's been a long time since I've seen you. I've been looking for you and I really missed you. Tell me all about what's been going on!" In this case Jim has responded with an overabundance of strokes. He has broken the rule. On the other hand, if Frank says, "Hi, Jim," and Jim ignores him, then Frank has given one stroke and not received one in response. That is called a stroke deficit. Again, Jim has broken the rule. Most people can stand only a small stroke deficit. If a person says, "Hi, Jim," three days in a row and Jim does not respond on any of those days, the individual quickly decides not to give any more strokes. Rituals are like a diet of celery—they momentarily appease hunger, but they never fully satisfy it. Most people need more intense strokes than rituals provide.

Pastimes

Pastimes are a means of structuring larger blocks of time. In "pastiming," people get and give strokes by discussing a topic of mutual interest. Pastimes also provide a means for getting to know people, establishing a position or image, or selecting partners for psychological games. "Where are you from?, What do you do?, and Ain't it awful?" are common pastimes. Pastimes are much like rituals in that they provide only weak strokes.

Activities

Activities structure the time people spend dealing with the world. Sometimes this involves processing information, solving problems, or talking out ideas with friends. All of these things are activities because the focus is upon making something happen in the real world. Stroking is a side benefit of activity.

Games

One of the most interesting approaches to organizing time is through games. A game is a process of give-and-take that moves toward a switch in roles by one or both persons. Games come in varying degrees of intensity. An example of a first-degree game is:

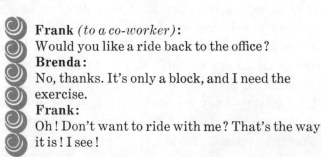

Frank *(to a co-worker)*:
Would you like a ride back to the office?
Brenda:
No, thanks. It's only a block, and I need the exercise.
Frank:
Oh! Don't want to ride with me? That's the way it is! I see!

Frank changed from rescuer to persecutor. That is the switch.

Games usually result in one or both parties storing up negative feelings and confirming negative beliefs about self and others. Fear and distrust are products of games. When six-year-old Andy asks his father for popcorn and then persecutes him because he is thirsty after eating the salty popcorn, that is a game.

A game always involves a switch in the roles of victim, persecutor, or rescuer. Cory asks Johnny where he was yesterday, taking the role of someone who wants to know. When Johnny says he was at woodshop, Cory switches roles to persecutor. "You were not. I saw you sneak out of school." As a result, both Cory and Johnny feel bad, and their negative beliefs are more deeply entrenched.

Games confirm a set of beliefs and feelings about who you are in the world. Some games support your feelings that you are inadequate—that you are not OK. They establish and maintain your own highly negative beliefs about the world. Other games are organized to blame others and to establish the belief that others are not OK. Games and their varying degrees of intensity are discussed in Chapter 6.

Positive Friendly Relationships
The final way of structuring time is through positive friendly relationships. In positive relationships, people share their feelings and beliefs in an accepting, trusting, and understanding way. Such relationships are especially important because they help people grow, learn, satisfy, and become satisfied. Positive friendly relationships constitute the high road to becoming OK. In other

ways of organizing time, people find social relationships that either fail to satisfy them fully or reinforce negative feelings and beliefs. In positive friendly relationships, people share themselves and their feelings; as a result, they bridge the chasm between themselves and others. In close relationships, conflict, distrust, negative feelings, and negative beliefs about the world fade. Closeness frees energy and allows people to live fully human lives and to feel, listen, trust, choose, respond, and create. It is through positive friendly relationships that people gain the emotional strength to be truly helping people. Such relationships involve a direct, honest, satisfying, and intense sharing between two or more people. In a friendly relationship, there is no exploitation or manipulation.

Consciously choosing to structure time in more positive and effective ways is a powerful tool in the process of becoming more OK. People relate to one another through a social contract. The social contract is a more-or-less conscious agreement between and among people to structure time in a given way. Individuals can choose a way of structuring time if they are conscious of their own needs and know how to initiate fruitful pastimes and more positive friendly relationships.

ASSESSING
TIME STRUCTURING

This exercise should help you find out the ways you structure your time. It may be done by yourself.

1 On what occasions do you find yourself "pastiming"? For example: (after work, at home, at parties, in the coffee lounge, while riding in a car.)

5 If you are an individual who has been aware of ritual patterns and have consciously changed your pattern in rituals, how so?

2 What are two of your most common pastimes? (What is the topic of conversation?)

3 What position do you establish with each of the two pastimes? (Are you a listener giving strokes? Do you want the other person to realize how much you know? Do you judge positively or negatively?)

6 In consideration of time structuring, it can be beneficial to think of the occasions when you have "time on your hands" (out-of-town business trips, at home alone). What do you do? Where do you like to go? Do you get involved in activities, pastimes, games, positive friendly relationships?

4 What is the most common manner in which you greet people? (Hi, hello, good morning, other.)

Psychological Trading Stamps

Eric Berne developed an analogy between the way people deal with their feelings and how they collect the trading stamps given for buying groceries or gasoline. A person gets trading stamps as a bonus for some legitimate transaction. That person saves the stamps until he or she gets some particular quantity of them, and then cashes them in for a prize. A person saves up feelings in the same way. The Parent tells the Child to save certain feelings. ("You are not supposed to show those feelings in public!") But an emergency clause comes with that injunction. If the feelings are strong enough, then the Child is allowed to show anger, cry, or withdraw. In much more serious situations, the Child might fall into a rage, demand a divorce, or even commit murder or suicide. The Parent ego state manages those feelings and allows a person to show them only on special occasions. The feelings reside in the Child part of the personality, and the Parent goes about the business of managing the behavior of the Child. Sometimes a contract is formed between the Child and the Parent. ("You may show those feelings only when they are built up.") Consider the following example:

> Mrs. Potter sometimes collects "anger stamps" on her eight-year-old son, Billy. From Mrs. Potter's first request to Billy to get up in the morning, through her demands that he finish his dinner, through homework in the evening, Mrs. Potter can control her feelings of anger in the same way she saves trading stamps. When the anger is built up enough, she cashes in the stamps by sending Billy to bed: "That's the last straw!

"GO TO BED!" Mrs. Potter's Parent allows her Child to express anger because her indignation has grown with all the events that occurred throughout the day.

Trading stamps, then, come from the internal dialogue between the Parent and the Child. The Parent says, "Don't vent anger." The Child complies until the feelings build up. The buildup of feelings justifies the Parent's permission to cash in the trading stamps for some prize. Consider this example:

Dick's Child urges him to overdrink. Dick's Parent does not allow this under normal conditions. Specifically, Dick's Parent says: "You can't drink too much because when you do, you hurt people who care about you." The Child then collects stamps when those who care about him make him angry. When enough anger has been stored in the Child, it justifies overdrinking. The Child says: "See, they don't care about me. I'm going to have a drink!" At that moment, the Parent loses control to the Child.

People collect different kinds of stamps. Some people collect all kinds of stamps. Most people have a favorite. Some people save up a number of stamps before cashing them in; others cash them in a page at a time. Common psychological trading stamps are anger and depression stamps.

Understanding stamps can help a person relate to others over a long haul. Do you collect stamps? What kind do you collect? Who is your favorite "redemption center"?

PSYCHOLOGICAL TRADING STAMP INVENTORY

Try answering
the following questions.

1 What is a psychological
   trading stamp?

2 What are some ways
   people collect stamps?

3 Why do you think people
   collect psychological
   trading stamps?

4 Who do people
   commonly use as
   redemption centers?

5 What kinds of prizes
   are there?

6 Do you think all stamps
   are legitimate?

7 Do you think everyone
   collects stamps?

8 Do you feel people
   can give up
   collecting stamps and give
   up their collection?

Transactions

transaction is a unit of social interaction comprised of an initiating message called the *stimulus* and a reply called the *response*. The stimulus and response might be verbal or nonverbal, but they must be received and acted upon by both parties. In other words, a transaction is some relationship between two people in which one says or does something and the other reacts. A transaction may involve any combination of ego states.

Transactions match or replay forms of interaction that develop early in life, such as, Parent-Child, Child-Child, or Adult-Adult. For instance, young children, when ordered about, become frightened or grumpy. Many years later, as grown-ups, they may get in a rut and replay the same transaction.

Transactions are diagramed to show from which ego states the stimulus and the response originate. For example:

Stimulus
Does anybody know what time it is?

Response
It's twenty after twelve.

An arrow is drawn from the ego state from which the stimulus originates to the ego state toward which the message is directed. An arrow in the other direction shows the response.

There are three basic kinds of transactions: complementary, crossed, and ulterior transactions.

Complementary Transactions

A transaction is complementary when someone aims a phrase, gesture, or action at another person and that person replies in the same ego state, as Parent, Adult, or Child. This means that someone trained in Transactional Analysis can predict responses in a series of complementary transactions. The following examples show different kinds of complementary transactions.

In the Adult-to-Adult transactions, information is exchanged, problems are analyzed, or decisions are made. Adult-to-Adult complementary transactions make up a large part of any activity. The key toward recognizing the Adult-to-Adult transaction is the rather unemotional exchange between the individuals.

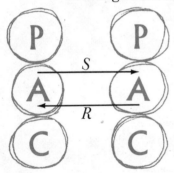

Stimulus
Can someone define
a preposition?

Response
A preposition
shows a relationship
between its object
and some other word
in the sentence.

Parent-to-Parent transactions are quite commonplace.

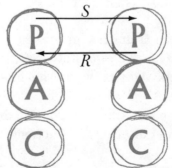

Stimulus
Those students
sure look terrible
with their long hair
and old patched jeans.

Response
They sure do.
And they don't respect
anything anymore.

50

In Parent-to-Parent complementary transactions, a judgment is often made about someone not present (in this case, the students), with both individuals in agreement. Judgments made in general statements and slogans are the key to identifying the Parent-to-Parent transaction. The judgment is sometimes positive and sometimes negative, and strings of these transactions can last for hours in a pastime.

Child-to-Child transactions are popular.

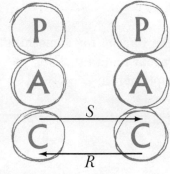

Stimulus
Hey! I really like you!
You're neat!

Response
And I think
you're absolutely super!

In this Child-to-Child transaction, both persons were in the Natural Child. The stimulus and response spontaneously expressed the joy, the openness of the Natural Child. While the Child-to-Child transaction might involve the Adapted Child—the Child developed in response to "parenting"—it is unlikely. The Adapted Child will tend to show itself in response to questions, orders, and nurturing from someone's Parent.

The Child-to-Parent transaction is common.

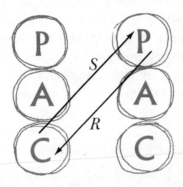

Stimulus
May I have some money
for a candy bar?

Response
Sure, here it is.

The Child asked the Parent for something, which was given. Even if the Parent had said, "No," the transaction would have been complementary.

The Parent-to-Child transaction is also very common.

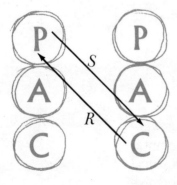

Stimulus
Go to bed! It's late.

Response
Couldn't I wait until
the end of the TV program?

The Parent spoke directly at the Child in the other person. In most such cases, the stimulus is aimed at the Child in order to gain compliance to some demand. The response came from the Adapted Child. This makes the transaction complementary by definition.

Sometimes the person in the Parent nurtures the other one:

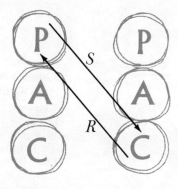

Stimulus
You are such a nice little girl.

Response
(nonverbal turn-on: smile, bright eyes.)

Parent-to-Child complementary transactions are common not only among parents and their children but also among grown-ups. Supervisor-trainee, husband-wife, teacher-pupil, doctor-patient, and many other grown-up relationships take this form. Sometimes the person thrust into the Child likes the role; sometimes not.

Crossed Transactions
Crossed transactions are some of the most interesting transactions. When Roberto asks, "Do you know where the toothpaste is?" and gets the response, "If you would only take care of things, you wouldn't have to ask me to keep track of them," he has been "crossed." The diagram of such a transaction looks like this:

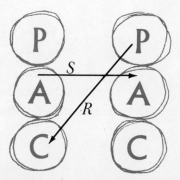

A crossed transaction occurs when the respondent reacts from a different ego state than the initiator aimed at. If the stimulus and response lines in a diagram are not parallel, the transaction is a crossed transaction.

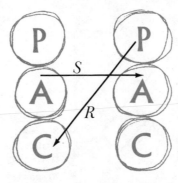

Stimulus
I need a hall pass
so I can go to the restroom.

Response
Oscar, you have five
minutes between classes.
You should have
used the restroom then.

An Adult stimulus started this transaction in a way similar to the first example. The response came from the Parent and was aimed at the Child. The transaction is crossed because the response did not come from the Adult.

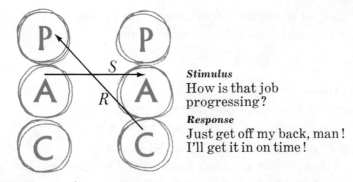

Stimulus
How is that job
progressing?

Response
Just get off my back, man!
I'll get it in on time!

The stimulus sought to get a reply from the Adult, but instead received a Child-to-Parent response. The crossed transaction is interesting and often leaves the initiator with his mouth hanging open in astonishment, anger, or pain.

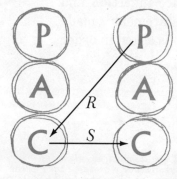

Stimulus
Let's ditch last hour and go shoot pool.

Response
You should know better than to do that.

The Child stimulus aimed at getting a Child response, such as, "Okay, let's go," but instead got a Parent response that made the transaction crossed.

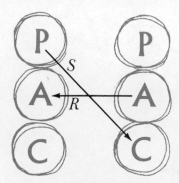

Stimulus
John, pick that paper up from underneath your desk.

Response
It was placed there by someone from second hour, but I'll help out and pick it up.

The Parent-to-Child stimulus aimed at and expected a Child response, but received an Adult response. Another crossed transaction.

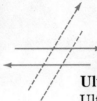

Ulterior Transactions

Ulterior transactions occur when one or both parties are functioning in two ego states at the same time. The words send one message while the voice inflection and gesturing send a different one. Often a statement is made in order to ask a question, or a question is asked in order to make a statement.

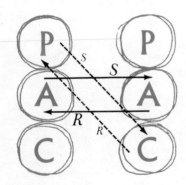

Stimulus

What time is it Paul? *The question was asked of a tardy student and sent the Parent message, "You shouldn't be late."*

Response

Oh, about 10:06, give or take a few seconds. *The answer sent the Child-to-Parent ulterior message, "Buzz off, it's not that big a deal."*

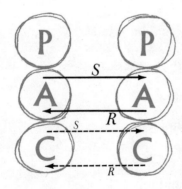

Stimulus *(with a groan)*

Hey, Pete, what time is it anyway? *The question sent the Child-to-Child ulterior message, "Sure wish this class was over."*

Response

It's only 10:06 *The response sent the Child-to-Child ulterior message, "Me, too!"*

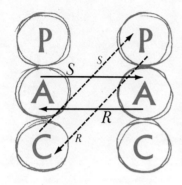

Stimulus *(in a coaxing tone)*
Mr. Bond is taking his classes outside today.

Response
Some teachers will do almost anything to win favor with their students.

The statement was made to the teacher and sent the Child-to-Parent message, "May we go outside, too?"

The response sent the Parent-to-Child ulterior message, "No, we can't go outside."

Using Transactions

Why is it important to know about transactions? The study of transactions is important in dealing with negative feelings aroused in your everyday relations with other people. It is important to understand what is happening in those relations so that you can consciously create ways of making those relations more positive, accepting, and understanding. This means being able to identify crossed and ulterior transactions. In crossed transactions, you will come to recognize where the cross comes from. And in ulterior transactions, you will be able to pick out the ulterior messages, bring them to the surface, and eventually be able to penetrate to an accepting and understanding relationship with the person who sends ulterior messages.

The following exercises will help you learn to analyze transactions.

DIAGRAMING AND CLASSIFYING COMPLEMENTARY AND CROSSED TRANSACTIONS

Draw the stimulus and response lines in each diagram and label each transaction as "complementary" or "crossed" on the line below each diagram. Begin each stimulus line from the personality on the left and each response line from the personality on the right.

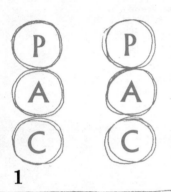

1

stimulus
I'm afraid I can't do it.

response
Don't worry. I'll be by your side to help.

2

stimulus
Hey! You're really a great-looking guy!

response
You shouldn't say things like that.

3

stimulus
What time is the faculty meeting?

response
Read the bulletin and you'll know.

4

stimulus
Joan is such a cute thing, and so sweet.

response
Yes, she's a wonderful person.

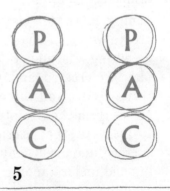

5

stimulus
You know better than that!

Response
Listen, Buster, it's the right thing to do!

58

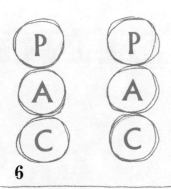

6

stimulus
Do you plan to mow the lawn
this weekend?

response
Why don't you get off my back
about the lawn?

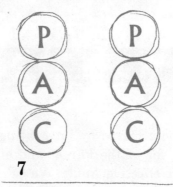

7

stimulus
Bet you a quarter I can
beat you to the corner.

response
I'll win hands down.
I'm the fastest in the world.

8

stimulus
Be careful! That knife
is sharp.

response
Okay, I'll watch it.
I'm always careful.

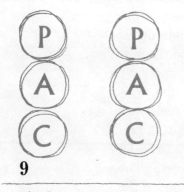

9

stimulus
I always have to do everything
around this house!

response
I've got a full-time job, too,
you know. Give me a break.

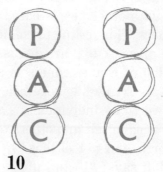

10

stimulus
Can you type these reports
by this afternoon?

response
What would you ever do
without me?

The statements made in the above transactions can
often be read in more than one way. For that reason,
more than one diagram for each set of stimuli and
responses may be reasonable and justifiable. The
following answers are suggestions only.

1 *stimulus* C to P
response P to C
complementary

2 *stimulus* C to C
response P to C
crossed

3 *stimulus* A to A
response P to C
crossed

4 *stimulus* P to P
response P to P
complementary

5 *stimulus* P to C
response P to C
crossed

6 *stimulus* A to A
response C to P
crossed

7 *stimulus* C to C
response C to C
complementary

8 *stimulus* P to C
response C to P
complementary

9 *stimulus* C to P
response C to P
crossed

10 *stimulus* A to A
reponse P to C
crossed

Chapter Five

THE FEELING

In the long run, OK-ness is achieved by integrating the feelings, beliefs, and behavior of the Parent and of the Adapted Child into a more effective Adult. We call this ego state the Feeling Adult. Most often the Adult ego state is described in terms of its information-processing, objective-appraising, and rational decision-making. All of these characteristics indicate that *feelings* are more a part of the other dimensions of the person—the Parent or the Child. The "Feeling Adult" suggests that in addition to processing, appraising, and making decisions, the Adult of the growing person also feels a sense of connectedness with other people based on new beliefs about self and others. This feeling of connectedness and the new beliefs that give rise to it are discussed in this chapter.

The feeling of connectedness is a reflection that we—you and I—are struggling together to grow, to feel more value and worth as individuals. The Feeling Adult recognizes the need in self and others to feel valued, to feel a sense of worth, and to feel that "I can take charge." The Feeling Adult says: "I can influence more and more the way I am behaving; I can act on the way I value myself as a person; I do not need to react *to*."

Responsibility Related to Growth

It is important to understand how responsibility is related to growth. But first, let us make a distinction between social, moral, or legal responsibility and the feelings of being responsible to or for other people. People often assume responsibility and feel responsible when there is no legal or moral responsibility. Similarly, people assume that others are responsible for them. It is a fact that

ADULT

parents, teachers, supervisors, doctors, lawyers, and citizens in general have legal responsibility to act in certain ways. These responsibilities are based upon the Constitution and upon local, state, and federal laws.

Some responsibility is not directly covered by laws but is moral, that is, it is generally recognized by people. Examples might be parents' responsibility to educate their children and citizens' responsibility to help keep the environment livable. The kind of responsibility that tends to limit growth is the legally and morally baseless feeling of responsibility we have to or for others. This feeling is based upon unrealistic beliefs held in the Parent and the Child.

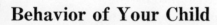 Behavior of Your Child

When Your Child sees the way others behave as saying something about itself that it does not like, Your Child tends to be defensive—it tends to reject the other person. When Your Child sees another behaving in a way that reflects affection, acceptance, and value, things run smoothly.

Your Child tends to look at others as being responsible for self. If things do not turn out, Your Child tends to resent the responsible person "because it was his or her fault." Your Child blames and rejects others and devalues others and self.

Your Child tends to see self as being responsible to others. "Tell me what to do; What do you expect of me?" are the Child's plea. When others fail to answer that plea, Your Child tends to think they deserve to be kicked, to be rejected, to be devalued. If someone tells you what to do, Your Child may feel resentful: "I don't have to if I don't want to. I don't want to be responsible to you."

Behavior of Your Parent

Your Parent tends to see others as responsible to self, that is, others should do what you expect. Your Parent also tends to see self as responsible for others, that is, you do things for people when they need help. Another way of viewing Your Parent is in the role of persecutor or rescuer. When other people are seen as responsible for meeting your expectations and they fail, Your Parent tends to persecute, to accuse others of being undependable or irresponsible. Such statements as "What is wrong with you?" or "You should know better than to do that" persecute or kick others. And kicking and persecuting someone does not contribute to his or her sense of worth.

Your Parent also tends to do things for others or to rescue them. When the Parent says, "Why don't you do this?" or, "You should do that!" or, "Be your own man and stand up for yourself," you are telling a person what to do. You are rescuing. You have taken responsibility for what others are doing or are about to do. If things work out well, others tend to value you more and themselves less. You rescued them—you did it for them. When things do not turn out well, the ones you attempted to rescue tend to kick you—"You told me to do it; It's all your fault;" or, "See what you made me do." You are responsible for them. They tend to value themselves more and you less. Your Parent, then, tends to look at others as behaving in a way that is in agreement with or contrary to what you expect of them. When other people's behavior

62

is in agreement with your expectations, you value them. When their behavior is contrary to your expectations, you reject them, think less of them, devalue them.

The two ways Your Parent tends to look at responsibility are: that others are responsible for meeting your expectations, and that you are responsible for others. One way, Your Parent persecutes others; the other way, Your Parent rescues them.

There are also many positive qualities of both Your Parent and Your Child which we have not discussed here.

The Integrated Person: The Feeling Adult

The Feeling Adult tends to look at self and others as mutually supportive and at the same time self-reliant. The sense of self-reliance—of personally searching for principles and codes of ethical conduct—is what makes the Feeling Adult more active as opposed to *re*-active. The Feeling Adult does not automatically react to people, situations, and the expectations of others. Rather, the Feeling Adult decides in a positive, social way how to react.

The Feeling Adult, by its general tone and quality, reflects connectedness with others in a warm-hearted, open, and sharing way. This connectedness—this understanding of the need to feel valued and the struggle to meet that need—brings about a new sense of sharing with others. Connectedness is the key to understanding others and growing with them in a mutually supportive way.

The Feeling Adult says, in effect: "Just as I need to feel valued, so do others." Self and others begin to be

63

looked upon as mutually supportive and at the same time self-reliant. Self-reliance increases as one recognizes the worth of self and others. Thus the Feeling Adult tends to negotiate rather than persecute, to facilitate rather than rescue.

In contrast to Your Child, who reacts defensively when people "say" things it does not like, the Feeling Adult looks at the way others behave as saying something about themselves, not about self. Even when the other person's behavior is negative or destructive, the Feeling Adult can sense the connectedness with that other person's struggle for self-worth. The Feeling Adult sees the other person as trying to come in contact with his or her own inherent value in order to put aside those negative feelings.

The Feeling Adult, then, is capable of information-processing, objective-appraising, and rational decision-making and, at the same time, has a sense of connectedness with others. The Feeling Adult believes that each person is primarily responsible for self and thus avoids the roles of rescuer, persecutor, and victim so characteristic of the Parent and the Child. The Feeling Adult recognizes that people have a strong need to affirm their own self-worth and inherent value and that when this recognition is made clear to others, a sense of closeness and togetherness replaces feelings of fear, hostility, and distrust. The Feeling Adult has an open, accepting, non-defensive way of relating to self and others.

 Each person can strengthen his or her Feeling Adult by becoming increasingly aware of self and others and by finding new ways to behave based on the belief that everyone who struggles to achieve self-worth is to be valued.

WHO IS RESPONSIBLE?

While there are legitimate social and legal responsibilities, this exercise looks at the way you feel about interpersonal responsibilities.

1
List the names of persons you feel responsible for and the feelings you experience with each person.

name

your feelings

a

b

c

2
List the names of persons you feel responsible to and the feelings you experience with each person.

name

your feelings

a

b

c

As you review your
feelings, try to pinpoint
your principal feelings—
those you experience
most often.

3
List the names of persons
you feel are responsible to you
and the feelings you
experience with each
person.

name

your feelings

a

b

c

4
List the names of persons
you feel are responsible for you
and the feelings you
experience with each
person.

name

your feelings

a

b

c

SORTING OUT FEELINGS, BELIEFS, AND BEHAVIORS

The purpose of this exercise is to develop skill in analyzing your feelings, beliefs, and behaviors in certain troublesome situations.

Think of a recent set of transactions that left you relating negatively toward someone. Ask yourself the following questions:

 How did I feel during the transactions?

 What beliefs do I have about myself, others, and the world in general that influenced how I felt and acted?

How did my actions relate to my feelings and beliefs?

 If I could have stepped outside myself, how would I have interpreted my own behavior?

Chapter Six

Games are

Games are ways of relating that involve people in one of three roles: persecutor, rescuer, or victim*. A persecutor relates by telling victims, both verbally and nonverbally, that they are bad, wrong, or inadequate in some way. A rescuer relates by doing for, or taking care of, victims, thereby telling them they are incapable of being self-reliant. A victim relates by asking for help, asking to be kicked, or allowing himself or herself to be kicked. Games occur as one or both parties change from one role to another. The result of changing roles is the rejection of others and the assigning of negative value to them. Relating through games contributes to isolation and valuing self and others less.

A sequence of relating through a game may go something like this: A person called the initiator, acting as victim or rescuer, makes a request to another person. The other person, called the responder, makes a response as victim or rescuer. Then one or the other changes roles to that of persecutor, and kicks. The result is rejecting and assigning negative value to the other person.

There is a tendency for some people to think the initiator is more at fault for relating through games than the responder. But the best way of looking at games is not to find either at fault. Both persons are relating as they have learned, and neither is fully aware or calculating. People do have the need to feel valued and of value; when they are not, they feel resentful and fearful. When people relate through games they feel less valued and of less value. But by relating in different ways, people can feel more valued and of more value.

Initiator makes a request by relating as victim or rescuer.

Responder makes a response by relating as victim or rescuing.

One person changes to relating as persecutor.

Both persons feel rejected and of less value.

*Known as the Karpman Drama Triangle.

ways of relating

Games that result in somewhat mild negative feelings are fairly socially acceptable and are classified as first degree. Even though somewhat mild, first-degree games cause people to move away from each other and think less of each other. When a game is considered not socially acceptable and the negative feelings are more intense, it is classified as second-degree. Third-degree games are extremely vicious and end in severe destruction, sometimes death. Some first- and second-degree games are described here. Some games may be played by more than two persons, but the following are limited to "two-handed" games.

See What You Made Me Do

A seven-year-old girl says to her father, "I just can't get the right color for this umbrella; I don't know what color to color it." The verbal statement is a description of the problem. The ulterior message sent is: "Please tell me what color I should color the umbrella."

Father responds, "Well, I sure like pink umbrellas. Pink is my favorite color. Why don't you color the umbrella pink?"

The girl colors the umbrella pink, but she decides it is a poor color. She stands up, takes the pink crayon, throws it against the wall, and cries, "See what you made me do!"

When the request is made for help in deciding what color the umbrella should be, the child relates as victim. The father relates by telling her what to do. He is the rescuer. After taking the advice, the child found that she didn't like the color. So she changed to relating as persecutor, saying, "See what you made me do; it's all your fault!" The father became victim.

If there is no change in roles, there is no game. If the child had taken the father's advice and said "Thank you" or had said "I don't like that pink color, but next time I'll try and color it a different color" without psychologically kicking or punishing the father, there would have been no game because there had not been a change in role. No rejection or negative feelings would have been assigned.

In the game *See What You Made Me Do*, the initiator manipulates the other person into being responsible for his or her behavior. The initiator is fearful or insecure, and asks for help in making a decision. After the responder has made the decision and that decision does not turn out, the initiator changes roles and says, in effect: "You were responsible for that decision and it's your fault, not mine." The initiator relates as victim; the responder relates as rescuer. After the change in roles, the initiator is the persecutor and the responder is the victim. People who respond to the initiating move in *See What You Made Me Do* are often people who need to feel helpful. They are rescuers. They are usually functioning in the Nurturing Parent and feel that in order to be an adequate friend, parent, or teacher, they need to help. Therefore they respond to the initiator's request for help by telling what to do.

A husband says to his wife, "Some people at the office have invited us to a dinner party in three weeks."

The day for the party arrives. That evening the wife says, "Well, I'm not too sure what to wear." The ulterior message is: "Please help me decide."

The husband responds and says, "Well, why don't you wear a long dress."

The wife agrees and they go to the party. She is the

70

only one there in a long dress. So she turns to the husband and says, "See what you made me do! I'm the only one here in a long dress. I feel out of place."

The wife believed the husband to be responsible for her. The wife initiated the game by relating as victim. The husband responded as rescuer. The wife changed to persecutor and the husband changed to victim. Both wound up feeling of less value.

If It Weren't for You

In the game *If It Weren't for You* the initiating move, the response, and the roles carried out on the parts of the initiator and responder are the same as in the game *See What You Made Me Do*. The difference between the two games is that in *See What You Made Me Do*, the responder has prescribed a certain behavior for the initiator. The father said to the daughter, "Why don't you color the umbrella pink?" The husband said to the wife, "Why don't you wear a long dress?" In both cases, something specific was suggested. In the game *If It Weren't for You*, the response is **don't** do this or **don't** do that. *If It Weren't for You* is preventing a person from doing something rather than telling the person to do something. When a person is prevented from doing something, he or she believes others are responsible; so the initiator-turned-prosecutor says, "If it weren't for you, I could have been a success; I would have made a fortune; I would have been popular." *If It Weren't for You* and *See What You Made Me Do* are, in a sense, complementary games. Here is an example of the former:

Child: Mark and Joan won't let me play with them.

Mother: Well, you just stay home and play with me, Honey. I told you not to play with those kids anyway. They're always trying to hurt you.

Fifteen minutes later the child changes from victim to persecutor.

Child: If it weren't for you, I could be out playing with the kids. You won't ever let me do anything!

Mother becomes victim; she is held responsible.

If the mother had said, "Well, you go out now and play with the kids. You've got to learn to get along with other children," the child may come back disappointed and discouraged. The child may then say, "See what you made me do! They still won't play with me." In order to avoid the traps of *See What You Made Me Do* and *If It Weren't for You*, the responder can facilitate rather than decide. How to facilitate is explained in the next chapter.

The game of *If It Weren't for You* between husband and wife might go something like this:

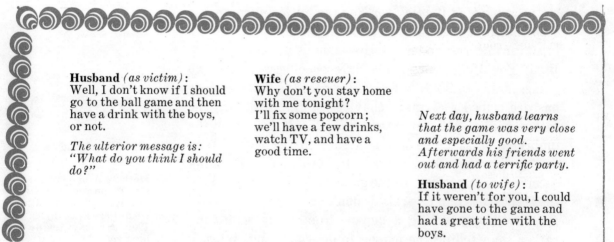

Husband *(as victim)*:
Well, I don't know if I should go to the ball game and then have a drink with the boys, or not.

The ulterior message is: "What do you think I should do?"

Wife *(as rescuer)*:
Why don't you stay home with me tonight? I'll fix some popcorn; we'll have a few drinks, watch TV, and have a good time.

Next day, husband learns that the game was very close and especially good. Afterwards his friends went out and had a terrific party.

Husband *(to wife)*:
If it weren't for you, I could have gone to the game and had a great time with the boys.

The game might even take another direction. During the evening of TV watching, regardless of the quality of the program, the husband might say, "Oh, what a terrible TV program! And you have too much butter on the popcorn and the drink's too weak. If it weren't for you, I'd be at the ball game having a good time."

Why Don't You...Yes, But

The game of *Why Don't You . . . Yes, But* is similar in nature to *See What You Made Me Do* and *If It Weren't For You*. In the two latter games, the initiator mentions a problem, the responder suggests how to solve it, and the initiator accepts the suggestion. However in *Why Don't You . . . Yes, But*, the initiator rejects the solution offered by the responder. Here is an example:

Wife: I'd like to go back to college and take some night courses.

Husband: Good idea! Why don't you do that?

Wife: Yes, but we don't have the money.

Husband *(relating as rescuer)*: Well, if we have the money for me to go to school, we have the money for you to do so.

Wife *(relating as victim)*: Oh, but I don't know how I'd get there. And we'd have to get a babysitter.

Husband: Why don't I go to school on Monday and Wednesday nights and you go on Tuesday and Thursday nights? That way we wouldn't have to get a babysitter.

Wife: Well, I don't know. Maybe! But it's still a long way there, and I don't want to drive at night by myself.

Husband: Say! Mary Ritter goes to school on Tuesday nights. You could ride with her.

Wife: Yes, but I don't have my transcripts yet, and I don't have an application.

Husband: Well, why don't I get your transcripts when I go over there? I'll also pick up application forms and you can fill them out here.

Wife: Maybe that's a good idea. But, oh, forget it. I'll handle it myself. Don't worry.

The wife was the victim who had the problem. The husband was the rescuer. In the end the wife changed and became the persecutor by saying, "Forget it. I'll handle it myself." That rejection moved the husband from the role of rescuer to that of victim. Both emerged with negative feelings.

Another example of *Why Don't You . . . Yes, But* involves a young boy with a problem who goes to a librarian, seeking a solution:

The boy is victim and poses the question: "What can I do? I can't find a book to read." The librarian is the rescuer and makes several suggestions. The boy finally rejects all the suggestions and so becomes the persecutor. The librarian becomes the frustrated victim.

Another variation of the game moves the librarian from rescuer to persecutor when she angrily says to the boy: "Well, you are just going to have to make up your mind, young man. And when you make up your mind, you come back to me. I don't have time to waste!" In this instance, the boy has remained victim.

Now I've Got You

In the game *Now I've Got You*, the initiating move is different from that in the previous three games. The initiating move sends ulterior messages; "I'm a rescuer. I'm about to accept you. I'm about to give you some very intense strokes." It also involves the message: "I accept you based upon certain conditions." The responder makes a move to meet those conditions in order to gain that acceptance and stroking. When the response is made, the initiator changes roles from rescuer to persecutor. The responder stays victim. A game of *Now I've Got You* might proceed along these lines:

Boy: I'm supposed to read a book for class and I don't know what to read.

Librarian *(relating as rescuer)*: Well, why don't you read a book about horses?

Boy: No, I don't like horses.

Librarian: How about a book about space? We have a lot of good space stories.

Boy: Naw, I see that on TV all the time. It's not very interesting.

Librarian: Oh, I've got it. I've got it! We just got this brand-new book in, and it's about ecology—about the pollution problem. How would you like to read that?

Boy: Oh, no, I read a book about that last year. Well, forget it. I'll try and find one myself.

Teacher *(relating as rescuer)*: John, I've been looking for you. I searched all over for you yesterday and couldn't find you anywhere. Where were you?

John: Gee, I was down in the shop making a table for my mom.

Teacher *(relating as persecutor)*: Oh, no, you weren't, John. I know exactly where you were. I saw you leaving school fifteen minutes early. You come with me to the principal's office. Now I've got you!

In this instance, the teacher pretended to be looking for John, even though he saw the student leave early. The student, thinking that the teacher wanted to give him some information or strokes, told a fib to keep from being rejected. But the teacher "got him"!

The initiator of *Now I've Got You* usually begins as the Nurturing Parent and changes to the Judgmental Parent—from rescuer to persecutor. The responder usually relates as victim, thinking he or she will be helped. Both persons experience negative feelings. The student is embarrassed and frightened or very resentful. The teacher is indignant and angry. Both also value the other less.

Usually people who relate through *Now I've Got You* have very strong Parental admonitions about right and wrong and the exact way of behaving. "It's wrong to leave early; It's wrong to fib; It's wrong to cheat." People relate as the Judgmental Parent in order to confirm the belief that others do bad things. The point of the game is to confirm the belief that people are no good because they cheat and fib. The individual who responds to the initiator of *Now I've Got You* is usually a corner-cutter. Corner-cutters often get caught in the game of *Now I've Got You* because they put things off and then fib to avoid Parental reprisals and the feeling of being valued less.

Here is another example:

The husband is angry. The wife feels mistreated. Both value each other less.

Husband *(relating as rescuer)*: Hi, dear. What did you do today?

Wife *(relating as victim)*: Not much. I wrote some letters. And I've been cooking a turkey on the grill.

Husband: So, you've been home all day, huh?

Wife: Yes.

Husband *(switching to persecutor)*: That's funny. I called at 2:05 and no one answered.

Wife *(flustered)*: I must have been talking to the next-door neighbor. I thought you meant did I go *out* anywhere.

Husband: Don't give me that. You knew what I meant. I never can trust you!

Rapo

apo involves sexual undertones and, in some situations, sexual contact. The initiator sends the message, "I'm available." The responder relates as victim by saying, "I need you, and I am glad you're available." The initiator then changes to persecutor, and kicks.

Two women are sitting together at a bar. Both are attractively dressed. Two men invite the women to have a drink with them. The women had sent the message, "We are available." The men had responded, "We are interested." After three drinks, one of the men asks one of the women, "Would you like to come home with me for a nightcap?"

The woman changes to persecutor and says, "Sure, I bet you would like that, wouldn't you? But I'm going home with my friend."

The kick was mild but firm. The woman feels indignant and the man feels inadequate—maybe even embarrassed or angry.

A man at a party is exchanging glances with someone who looks interesting. Later that evening the woman comes up to him and says, "I've noticed you this evening. Are you new in town?"

"Yes, I am," responds the man in a very friendly tone.

"I'm having a couple over for breakfast after the party. Can you make it?" she asks.

"I don't think my wife would like that very much," the man answers.

The man initially related as rescuer ("I'm available"). The woman responded as victim, taking him up on his ulterior offer. The man then changed to persecutor.

Rapo is often a test to see who will make the responding

move to the other person. While both persons are sending the ulterior message, "I'm available," both are waiting to see who will respond. Once that response is made, the other person is in a position to change his or her way of relating to persecutor, and kick. Sexual contact usually intensifies the game, but the roles and changes occur in much the same sequence.

A person relating through *Rapo* as persecutor may either think sex is bad or evil, or may think the other person is inferior and should be kicked. The victim feels rejected and inadequate. Both value each other less and continue to believe the same things about other people and about sex.

Kick Me

Kick Me follows roughly the same sequence as *Now I've Got You* and *Rapo*. In *Now I've Got You*, the initiator, relating as rescuer, has a piece of concealed information about the other person which is revealed in the role of prosecutor after the responder relates as victim to the rescuing move. In *Rapo* the initiator, relating as rescuer, sends an "I'm available" message which is changed to "You read the wrong thing, buster" after the victim responds to the rescuing offer. In *Kick Me*, the initiator relates as rescuer by indicating that he or she will do this or that for the other person. The responder relates as victim, saying, "Thanks for the help." The initiator either procrastinates and never does what was promised, or does not do what was promised adequately. The victim then changes to persecutor, and kicks. The initiator is victim.

Here is an instance of how *Kick Me* might proceed:

Wife: *(relating as rescuer)*: I'll be glad to take the car to the garage today if you're busy. I plan to go to town anyway.

Husband: Thanks! That will be a help. The right rear shock is loose. The tires need rotating and the oil should be changed. Also, I think we had better get the engine tuned up for the weekend trip.

Next day, pulling out of the driveway, the husband notices that the right rear shock rattles. He turns angrily to his wife.

Husband: Can't you do anything right? I told you to have that shock tightened.

Wife: But, I thought I told them to. I must have forgotten.

Husband: *(relating as persecutor)*: Sure, you did! You're always messing things up.

The hurt wife sits in silence as the negative feelings settle in. The husband is frustrated. Both persons value each other less.

It must be stressed that games are learned ways of relating. But people can also learn to relate through facilitating, negotiating, and initiating. These new ways of relating will be discussed in subsequent chapters. They can influence the way you relate. They can also be the vehicle for valuing yourself and others more and for creating joy in your interpersonal relationships.

THE GAMES I RELATE THROUGH

rescuer
persecutor
victim
feeling adult

List
the names
of persons
that you are currently
relating with.

If possible
describe each person
as rescuer, persecutor, victim,
or Feeling Adult.*

Next to that description
write how you relate
with that person,
using the same descriptors.*

1

2

3

4

5

6

7

8

9

10

*Both you and the other person
may relate
in more than one way.

THE GAMES I RELATE THROUGH
continued

Using the same descriptors,
describe how you think
the other person
sees you relating.*

Describe how you and the other person feel.
There may be several feelings.
Choose the two that occur most frequently
when you are relating with each other.

1

2

3

4

5

6

7

8

9

10

*You may relate
in more than one way.

Using this information,
can you see games that you relate through?
If so,
name the person you relate with
and the game.

name   *game*

1
_____

2
_____

3
_____

4
_____

5
_____

6
_____

7
_____

8
_____

9
_____

10
_____

from RESCUING

The term "rescuing" means doing something for someone or giving advice about what to do. Rescuing is assuming responsibility for someone else. If the advice you give is accepted by the other person, you may be blamed later or made to feel guilty because you are taking on responsibility for the other person. The games that commonly involve you relating as rescuer are initiated by the other person relating as victim. The victim then changes roles to persecutor. In this chapter you will find out how to relate as a facilitator so that you don't become responsible for someone else and so that, at the same time, you help the other person grow.

Some people think that relating as rescuer is a helpful way to act toward another person. The authors, however, think that rescuing hinders growth because people learn to count on it—it creates dependency. Facilitating rather than rescuing promotes growth because it creates self-reliance. In facilitating, you respond to the victim in the Feeling Adult in a warm-hearted, exchanging way that helps the victim solve his or her problem or make his or her own decision. As the victim begins to make his or her own decision, he or she begins growing in self-reliance and in self-worth and moves away from dependency and self-abasement.

A facilitator understands that growing means becoming more self-reliant and valuing self more. When a person expresses fear or insecurity about something or someone, or wonders what to do, the facilitator relates by touching base with the feelings of the other person. When touching base with feelings is not sufficient to allow another to gain self-reliance, the Feeling Adult can continue to facilitate by clarifying what the other person wants

to **FACILITATING**

to do, exploring the ways it might be done, and developing a plan for acting.

In summary, facilitating can involve these ways of relating:

1. Touching base with feelings
2. Clarifying what the other person wants to do
3. Exploring ways of doing what the other person wants to do
4. Developing a plan of action

P Touching Base with Feelings

Part of touching base with feelings is understanding that feelings are connected to something—they do not arise out of the blue. Feelings arise out of each person's experiences and the ways each person has of interpreting his or her experiences. Describing a feeling is different from evaluating a feeling.

Decribing A Feeling

Describing a feeling is saying that it is OK to feel that way. "I realize that you are human and that, in being human, you have feelings. Your feelings may be tied to things that are different from the things my feelings are tied to, but that is OK. Your feelings of frustration might be produced by different events than mine are, but they are tied to events. Your feelings of disappointment might be tied to something different than my feelings of disappointment. But it is OK to feel disappointment, regardless of why you feel disappointment. I unconditionally recognize that feeling."

Evaluating A Feeling

When you evaluate a feeling, you send the message: "You shouldn't feel that way in light of that situation or in light of that event. It is silly to feel disappointed because that person didn't want to go out with you." Evaluating feelings is sending the message: "I don't accept you." It says, "Your feeling is not legitimate." We often evaluate our own feelings: "It is silly of me to feel discounted. I am sure that person didn't mean to say that. Or perhaps what I heard is not what he meant." Learning to accept feelings in ourselves is crucial to becoming OK. It occurs when we understand that our feelings are tied to things and to people and when we learn to associate a certain feeling with a particular event or person.

Connectedness Through Touching Base with Feelings

The following are some examples of touching base with feelings:

Child: Those kids won't let me play jump rope!

Facilitating mother *(in a warm, accepting way)*: And that hurts you.

Student: I want to be a mechanic, but my dad thinks I should go to college or I won't amount to anything.

Facilitating teacher *(in a warm, affirming tone)*: And that makes you feel trapped and pressured.

The words "hurt," "pressured," and "trapped" are feeling words. The facilitating person listens to and watches for the indicators of feelings and then reflects them and describes them. That process shows connectedness through touching base with feelings.

The Feeling Adult not only uses the information-processing and objective-appraising capacity but also the capacity to feel connectedness. Connectedness in the Feeling Adult can also be shared in positive feelings, for example:

Child: Oh! This summer I went to the ocean and saw the biggest ship in the world. It was the giantest ship ever.

Facilitating grandfather *(in an excited, accepting tone)*: It must have really been exciting and thrilling to see such a huge ship.

The feeling was identified in kind and intensity. The particular experience that it was associated with was also identified. Stating the feeling and describing it with the same intensity as the child did amounts to measuring the feeling. It communicates understanding: "I know what it is to feel that way." It communicates connectedness.

Touching base with feelings can be sufficient in some situations for the other person to say: "Yes, it does hurt, but I guess I'm too little to play jump rope" or "Yes, I do feel trapped, but I think Dad and I can work things out."

Clarifying What the Other Person Wants to Do

Rescuing focuses on what you think the other person ought to do about his or her situation. Facilitating focuses on what the other person wants to do. Facilitating is believing that each person is capable of solving his or her own problems. Of course, many people do not solve their own problems. But this is probably because they have been rescued and do not know how to solve them. Facilitating aims at clarifying what the person wants to do about his or her situation. The facilitating mother could have done this by saying: "And you want to be included so that you can play jump rope." The facilitating teacher might have been able to "read" what the student would like, and say: "You would like to work it out so that you could be a mechanic and still have your dad value you." If there is doubt about what the other person wants to do, one can always ask: "What would you like to do about that?"

It is important to avoid choosing sides in a conflict situation between the problem person and someone else. By choosing sides, you set the goal and run the risk of relating as rescuer, and being blamed. Choosing sides in a situation might sound like this:

Rescuing mother gives advice and moves toward **See What You Made Me Do:** "You must learn to play with others. Now, go try again."

Rescuing mother takes the side of the child and moves toward **If It Weren't for You:** "You stay with me. I'll play with you."

*Rescuing teacher takes side of Dad and moves toward **If It Weren't for You:** "Your dad loves you and wants only to help you. Go to college! It will be good for you."*

*Rescuing teacher takes the side of the student and moves toward **See What You Made Me Do:** "Go to your dad and tell him that it is your life. He can make decisions about his own life, but he can't make decisions about your life."*

Clarifying what the other person would like to do avoids relating as rescuer and relating through games.

The Feeling Adult believes that the other person has the inherent right to decide what to do about his or her situation. That does not mean that the child can attack other children or yell at Mother. But within limits the person can choose to do what he or she wishes as long as he or she does not impose his or her values on another. The tone of that belief is reflected in the connectedness of the Feeling Adult and in the effort to clarify what the problem person wants to do about his or her situation.

Exploring Ways of Doing What the Other Person Wants to Do

Facilitating involves relating as a mutual explorer with the problem person in seeking for ways to do what the person wants to do. Mutually exploring means that you and the other person talk about ways of realizing the goal. Together you predict what you think might happen with each way of trying to realize the goal. Of course, the future cannot really be predicted; but looking at what you think might happen can avoid some costly emotional mistakes.

Returning to the example of the facilitating mother, we can examine some possible responses to the child who has been rejected by playmates. Rather than give advice, the mother might ask the child what could be done: "What do you think you might do so that the other kids will allow you to play with them?" If the child has no suggestions, the mother might offer some:

 "What do you think about telling the other kids: 'I really like to play jump rope, and it hurts me when I can't' or 'If you show me how to play jump rope, I'll try hard to do it right.'?"

If the child responds negatively to the suggestions, the mother can try others. Should the child continue to reject suggestions and begins to move toward *Why Don't You . . . Yes, But,* the mother can be supportive and say some such things as:

 "I can tell you aren't sure about what to do. After you think about it, I'll be glad to talk with you some more. I'll be in the den reading."

Facilitating, in this situation, is touching base with indecision.

In the example of the facilitating teacher and the student, a dialog might proceed like this:

 Facilitating teacher: How do you think you might go to school to become a mechanic and at the same time have your father value you?

 Student: I'm not sure. I've thought of going to a community college where I could do both.

The student has chosen a fairly practical way of achieving his goal and can be supported by the facilitating teacher. Facilitating might now move to exploring which community college to attend or how to discuss the community-college idea with the student's father. How to implement the chosen solutions leads to developing a plan of action.

Developing a Plan of Action

Facilitating often stops before a plan of action has been developed. In some cases that might be appropriate. But it is important that the person with the problem make the decision as to whether or not he or she feels self-reliant enough to carry out a plan without the facilitator.

Facilitating a plan of action can involve charting the plan or even role-playing the situation. The facilitating mother role-played when she acted out what her child might say to the children playing jump rope. The facilitating teacher could role-play the father in the situation where the student suggests the idea of going to a community college. One important thing to remember in role-playing a plan of action: control the tone of communication so as to avoid relating as victim, rescuer, or persecutor.

Facilitating, in summary, is a way of relating that promotes self-reliance and at the same time gives mutual support. The Feeling Adult can relate warmly and genuinely through facilitating by sharing connectedness with others.

BECOMING AWARE
OF FEELINGS

Many people have difficulty touching base with feelings because they never really attend to others. They never really see the evidences of feelings because they never really look. The following are some suggestions to help you become more aware of feelings—both your own and others'.

 1

The next time you are in a room full of people, pick out two or three individuals and see if you can describe to yourself their feelings.

 2

Can you identify those people with an open, accepting posture? What are their feelings? Can you identify those people with a closed, defensive posture? Does everyone in the group fit into one classification or the other?

 **3**

Can you remember how you sat, stood, and moved the last time you were angry? How about the last time you were very pleased with yourself?

 4

Are you uncomfortable around some particular person? What is your body language around that person?

THE FEELING VOCABULARY

The range of human feelings seems
almost endless. Touching base with feeling means that we use a feeling word
to reflect the feeling of others.
This presents a problem.

Many, probably most, of us
do not have a large enough vocabulary
of feeling words to accurately reflect feelings. In the space below,
list as many feeling words as you can.

Continue to record feeling words
as they come to you.

EXERCISE IN FACILITATING

Your ten-year-old son comes in from
school on the verge of tears
and says: "That Mrs. Adams,
she never lets us do anything!
All I did was talk to Jim for one minute.
He talked first, and she made *me* stay
after school for talking."

Try to give a response
that touches base
with your son's feelings.

Make up a response
for your son.

Now, clarify
what he wants to do.

Make up another response
for your son.

Now, try to explore
what your son might do
to reach his goal.

Make up a response
for your son.

Now, help develop
a plan of action.

Chapter Eight

from persecuting

Persecuting, or kicking, in a psychological sense aims at establishing blame or fault. Both the Parent and the Child persecute. Shouting angrily or sending nonverbal messages of blame or resentment is persecuting. Relating through persecuting is a learned way of behaving; however, negotiating can replace it as a new way of relating that leads people to value themselves and others more. This chapter is about negotiating. Increasing your skill in negotiating is the aim of this chapter.

Touching Base with Feelings and Establishing Guidelines

We think that anger is learned, that usually a person becomes embarrassed, hurt, worried, frustrated, or disappointed—and then angry.

In the following example, a father and mother have been pacing the floor, worried sick that their daughter—out on her first date—has been hurt. It is 12:30 A.M., and the daughter had agreed to be home at 12:00. As she walks in, the father shouts at her angrily:

Father: Where have you been, young lady? I have a mind to give you a spanking. You're not too big for that, you know!

Daughter *(shouting)*: I'm just a little late, Dad! Why do you always pick on me?

to negotiating

The point is that the father was worried and concerned, but he expressed anger instead. He was relating to his daughter as persecutor.

In negotiating this situation, the father might have said: "I'm so glad you are home! I have been so worried about you! The next time you'll be later than we agreed upon, call and let me know so I won't be worried. Now, did you have a good time?" This is the kind of thing Tom Gordon recommends in his book, *Parent Effectiveness Training*. Gordon describes the above kind of statement as an "I statement." The "I statement" describes *my* feelings, rather than placing blame or persecuting the other person.

Negotiating rather than persecuting involves touching base with your initial feelings and then setting guidelines for future situations so that negative feelings can be avoided. In most instances, those guidelines can be set by mutual decision. When guidelines are set by mutual agreement, both parties share in the feeling of responsibility, and both parties feel a sense of connectedness and mutual value. In the above situation, one can assume that the daughter agrees to the suggestion of calling the next time she will be late. If she does not, another guideline could be agreed upon.

For individuals who relate as victim, negotiating can also be a powerful tool. The wife who was persecuted because she was not home at 2:05 when her husband called might say: "I look forward to your calling. You might try several times if it is important." The statement is direct, warm, and exchanging, indicating that the relationship is important.

A person relating as victim changed to relating as negotiator in the following incident.

Several days after a get-together, a woman approached the host in a public place and said in a loud voice: "I felt excluded at your house the other night. I'll bet the other women did, too. You paid no attention to us!"

The host could take the kick and let the issue slide by, merely saying: "I'm sorry. I didn't mean to exclude you." He could also become defensive and relate by saying: "Buzz off! I didn't exclude you on purpose. You're a big girl. Why didn't you say something that night?"

Both of the above responses contribute to negative feelings and cause the individuals to value themselves and each other less. Relating through negotiating might sound like this:

Host: It's important to me not to discount you. When you feel excluded again, let me know, because I value you.

Woman: All right, I will. I was afraid you would be defensive and kick me. I'm glad you didn't.

Both of these statements are warm and conciliatory. As Feeling Adults, the individuals expressed connectedness with each other in a positive, exchanging way.

Summarizing the Art of Negotiating

The two suggestions about negotiating that have been made so far are:

---

1 Touch base with the initial feeling in yourself or in the other person. When you do so, describe the feeling in words such as: "I'm hurt; I'm frustrated; I'm concerned; I'm disappointed." Such descriptions indicate that you believe that you are responsible for the way you feel.

---

2 Try to establish guidelines for new ways of relating.

Call me next time you will be late.

Let me know when you feel excluded again.

If the guidelines you set are not acceptable, let the other person set them. The important thing is to mutually establish guidelines for a relationship, because each person in the relationship has the inherent right to contribute equally. One very important thing that psychologists seem to agree upon is the timing of guidelines. They should be set in advance, not after the fact. Setting them after the fact is *Now I've Got You*. Guidelines should also continuously change as the relationship changes. Relating as persecutor maintains a role that prevents change. So does relating as victim.

Negotiating is relating with the understanding that you and the other person change, and that you both value your connectedness with each other. Negotiating is increasingly recognizing the inherent value of yourself and the other person as you grow more self-reliant and, at the same time, mutually supporting.

The following example shows how a teacher negotiates with a rebellious student:

Student: I hate that stupid math! I'm not going to do it!

Negotiating teacher: It's frustrating to have to do something you don't feel like doing.

Student: You bet! And I'm still not going to do it.

Negotiating teacher: That is your choice, Frankie. If you change your mind, let me know. I will try to work it out with you so that your math assignment won't be so frustrating and you won't hate it so much.

The negotiating teacher recognizes that her role is not to persecute Frankie and force him to do his math. It is to negotiate in a warm and genuine manner, indicating that she values him and that it is all right to feel frustrated and to dislike doing math.

The Feeling Adult recognizes the inherent value of choosing for oneself. You cannot chose for others, but neither can others choose for you. That means Frankie can choose not to do math, but he cannot choose to interfere with others doing math. Neither can he choose to kick the teacher because he feels frustrated doing math. Within that framwork, guidelines can be mutually agreed upon.

Negotiating breeds negotiating. It is continuous. It is a way of relating. It is a way of recognizing inherent value in self and others.

NEGOTIATING

This exercise is provided to help you look at the skills involved in negotiation. You are required to furnish the situation. Think of any situation in which you will have to negotiate. This might be an occasion when you have made a mistake or someone else has made one. Answer the questions for yourself.

1

Have you played persecutor or victim in this situation?

2

Can you make a statement disclosing your initial feelings about this situation? Begin your statement: *I feel ...*

3

If this situation arises in the future, what would you like to have happen?

4

Can you suggest some guidelines so that the needs of both parties can be met? Begin your statement: *I suggest that ...*

from ISOLATING

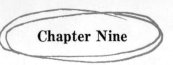

As people begin to think more clearly about themselves and their relationships with others, two problems or concerns outweigh all others. The first is that many people, both young and old, are lonely—sometimes so lonely that they feel life has no meaning for them. The second is that people just do not know how or where to start the process of growing. Coping with loneliness and growing are part of the same process.

In the previous chapters, we have discussed a series of beliefs, feelings, and behaviors that lead to isolation of the individual. The basic theme has been that each of us has three relatively distinct ego states.

The Parent ego state is basically the recordings of our own interpretations of our parents' behavior. It is highly judgmental and directive; it is responsible for others and expects others to be responsible to it.

The Child ego state reflects the basic biological and psychological needs as well as the recordings of feeling responses set up early in childhood. Many of those recorded responses are incomplete and hinder growth in grown-up life.

In the Adult ego state, the individual behaves in effective ways, both in interpersonal relationships and in satisfying his or her own needs. We call this the Feeling Adult.

We have discussed the isolating behavior of role-playing. The rescuer, victim, and persecutor are characteristic ways of relating that result in individuals feeling depen-

to INITIATING

dent on, of little value to, angry at, and negative toward one another. In fact, these roles hinder growth. We have also looked at isolating behavior in terms of communication—people speaking in indirect ways and sending negative and discounting ulterior messages. And we have seen that relating through games ultimately results in feelings of alienation rather than connectedness.

The goal toward which growing people move requires openness, acceptance of others, and a valuing of self and others in a nonmanipulative way. It involves ways of relating to other people that convey to them positive valuing messages rather than destructive discounting messages.

Initiating is a set of skills based upon the beliefs in the Feeling Adult that each person has inherent value and that each needs to feel of value and to be valued. The message that "I value you" must be communicated significantly and clearly to you in order for you to feel open and accepting. Such messages help you experience the feeling of connectedness with other people. Connectedness is the feeling of closeness, of participation with other human beings. It is the feeling that in social relationships both people can win. My winning, my sense of being OK, is not dependent upon your losing. The feeling of connectedness is also related to a sharing of common needs and a recognition that everyone needs to be treated fairly and positively.

Initiating and the Social Contact

The theory of Transactional Analysis is based upon the assumption that all of us have needs for recognition and stimulation that we satisfy through social interaction. We structure our time in order to satisfy our needs, and we communicate our needs and expectations to other people in many ways. As discussed before, we structure our time in one of six ways: withdrawal, rituals, pastimes, activities, games, or positive friendly relationships. We initiate our relationships with others by sending and receiving cues about the way we expect to relate to them. Our posture, gestures, and tone of voice can send the message: "This is a two-stroke ritual" or "Let's talk a while."

Initiating positive relationships with other human beings involves a set of skills and attitudes, the first of which is self-awareness. This means that we must be aware of our own needs—social, physical, and psychological. We must be aware of the way we are behaving. Initiating also involves the skill of self-disclosure. We must be able to communicate ourselves, our needs, our hopes, our desires, our feelings, and our values to other human beings in open and nonsecretive ways. Because we have been involved in games and have related with others through games, self-disclosure includes a measure of risk-taking. Initiating also involves the skill of assessing other people's needs, feelings, wishes, and desires. When a person has achieved these skills, initiating becomes a relatively simple task.

When people who have not previously known each other come together in a casual way, they tend to relate through rituals or pastimes. Rituals often involve a very mild stroking, not an intensely positive stroking. Pastimes establish a social position and a way of exchanging mildly positive strokes. Rituals can involve a genuine acceptance of the other human being. They can communicate trust, with the message, "I value you." Pastimes often involve us in competitive kinds of structures: "My toys are better than your toys;" "I'm in competition with you;" "Ain't it awful?" (meaning "It's you and I against the world "). Pastimes can also be used to convey the positive messages of trust, acceptance, and valuing.

No one way of acting leads automatically to close, positive feelings of connectedness. Initiating is one of the ways of acting that help lead to acceptance and understanding. Initiating is:

- recognizing worth and value in self and others.
- reaching out to touch someone.
- disclosing your own feelings.
- taking a chance, a risk, that you will be misunderstood or rejected.
- facilitating, not rescuing.
- talking over important things.
- overcoming the fears of Your Child.
- bypassing the restrictions of Your Parent.
- spontaneously touching base with feelings.
- having a sense of trust in self and others.
- reading others—seeing what they feel, want, and need.
- knowing that others need intense, positive strokes— and giving them.
- knowing that anger comes from hurt, from exclusion.
- sharing yourself, your feelings, your needs.
- talking to someone who is lonely.

CREATIVE FANTASY

Time and time again, people say such things as: "Sometimes I know that what I am saying or doing (or not saying or doing) is not the best thing. But at that time I didn't know what to say or do. After the fact things always seem simpler, and I can think of ways of responding that probably would have worked."

"Creative Fantasy" is an exercise in which you think of responses and actually build them into your automatic set of responses.

In the following situations, imagine yourself responding in definite and positive ways. Say aloud to yourself the things you would say in the situation.

Situation I

In this situation, you come face-to-face with someone you know but would like to know better. You are on a bus, and the person sits next to you.

I would say:

Yesterday you had an argument with a friend. Today is the first time you have seen the friend since the argument.

I would say:

You work with a person who has a habit that drives you crazy. You would like to tell the person about the annoying habit, and you finally get a chance to talk with him or her.

I would say:

Contracting and Recontracting

Sometimes people who have been very close to one another drift apart. Somehow the relationship changes and the people involved feel that there is a barrier between them. Many people are able to discuss problems more easily with a relative stranger than with a former intimate friend. They feel that it takes too much courage to discuss a problem with the person involved. It is a tough problem. We must look at it, analyze it, and build ways of dealing with it through the idea of recontracting.

An interpersonal contract is an agreement between two or more people to act toward each other in relatively specific and predictable ways. Each person gets the benefit of security in return for acting in certain ways. An interpersonal contract is much like a legal contract. Each person agrees to structure time in certain ways, to play certain games, and to *not* notice or talk about certain aspects of the other person's behavior. Like a legal contract, the interpersonal contract might be consciously defined and agreed upon by both parties, as is the case with some wedding contracts; or, it might have a lot of "fine print" to which each party agrees, even though neither is fully aware of nor fully understands the fine print.

People in sales work are very much aware that after individuals sign a sales contract they often have second thoughts. The deal often does not look so good the morning after. The purchaser feels that because of the excitement of the sales and the anticipation of the benefits of the purchase, he or she has paid too high a price. In sales, it is often too late at that point to rewrite the contract. In interpersonal relationships, the stakes are too high to *not* rewrite the contract. Continually rewriting the inter-personal contract is crucial to on-going personal growth.

Time and people change.

Contracts get out of date. Some contracts allow for change and growth in both parties; others do not. The "good" contract is one that is written with growth in mind. When this is done, people who feel that their needs are not being met—who are alienated and separated from the people they love—can revitalize the relationships and recapture the feelings they once had.

When you cannot talk freely to someone close to you, it is time to recontract. In recontracting a new, more con-scious, more need-fulfilling and "growthful" contract is agreed upon.

Sometimes contracts are lopsided, giving the major benefit to one party or the other. The following contract between Charlie and Maude is a good example of a lop-sided contract. This contract is written only in general terms. A real contract would be more complex.

Charlie and Maude have been married for eight years.
This is their original contract:

Charlie promised to	In return Charlie expects to	Maude promised to	In return Maude expects to
: go out into the world and work for a living.	: rest when he comes home and not be bothered by "little things."	: take care of the house and children.	: have protection from the world.
: be *relatively* faithful to Maude.	: have the last and unquestioned word on family decisions.	: take care of Charlie's physical needs.	: get companionship from Charlie.
: not discuss Maude's weaknesses and fears in front of others.	: not be questioned about his job.	: love, honor, and cherish Charlie (especially in public).	: enjoy relative faithfulness from Charlie.
: provide companionship at certain times.	: be able to collect and cash in anger stamps on Maude.	: provide companionship for Charlie.	: keep Charlie as "my man."
	: be sexually satisfied when he so desires.	: put up with Charlie's "ways" without complaint.	: play *If It Weren't for You.*
	: be treated as a "real man" in public.		
	: go hunting with the "boys" for one week each year.		
	: play *See What You Made Me Do.*		

There are several immediate observations to be made about this contract:

 1
Charlie seems to be getting
the best of Maude,
at least by current standards.

 2
The contract was written
to satisfy both Charlie's
and Maude's urgent
but relatively short-term needs
for security, strokes,
and gratification rather than
to promote their long-term
growth.

 3
The contract was written
to preserve a way of relating
that will cause both Charlie
and Maude to maintain
negative beliefs
about self and others.

 4
The contract was based upon
cultural stereotypes
of the role of the male
and the female in marriage.

After eight years of marriage the urgency of both Maude's and Charlie's needs for security and for constant companionship diminished. Maude began to be increasingly irritated and frustrated by Charlie's aloofness from family management. She saw an increasing responsibility for herself in dealing with the growth of the family and thought that Charlie should share more of that burden. She also felt lonely and excluded when Charlie went on his annual hunting trip. Maude used *If It Weren't for You* to communicate her feelings to Charlie. That game caused Charlie to collect more anger stamps and to cash them in on Maude by being sullen and withdrawn.

Clearly the contract, out of the urgency of loneliness that both Charlie and Maude felt, became more and more inadequate and troublesome. The contract that had helped them develop some predictability in their relationship was no longer adequate. It was past time for Maude and Charlie to recontract. Maude and Charlie were lucky enough to talk with a professional, who helped them understand what had happened and assisted them in gradually building a more effective contract.

Charlie and Maude went through three basic steps in recontracting:

1
Each partner
had to clarify
what he or she needed
from the relationship.

2
Both Charlie and Maude
had to clarify
the existing contract.

3
A new, more effective,
agreement or
understanding
had to be drawn up.

As Charlie and Maude examined what they needed from the relationship, Charlie decided that what he needed most was still the security of knowing that Maude loved him. Another part of Charlie needed to play the role of protector in order to maintain his sense of self-worth. When Charlie told Maude that, a lot of her negative feelings subsided and she agreed that she also needed security and reassurance of her self-worth. But Maude also said she needed some time away from the role she had been playing. For Maude, Charlie's aloofness from

110

household problems and his annual hunting trips sent her a discounting message. Maude could not feel secure and valued, and be discounted at the same time. For Maude, knowing Charlie's need to play the role of protector helped her understand some of the things that had been happening.

After long discussion, Charlie suggested that he might either cut his annual hunting trip to a couple of days or cut it out altogether. He felt that if he cut the trip out altogether, he would lose some prestige with his friends. Maude said that she would feel better about things if he would simply cut the trip to a couple of days a year. They agreed to try one two-day hunting trip, and then to discuss that point again.

This left two other major trouble spots—the games that they both played and Maude's feelings about Charlie's part in the household. The game-playing was reduced and finally eliminated as both partners began to see how the games worked to keep negative feelings stirred up and how the rescuer, victim, and persecutor roles had kept them engaged in the game. As Charlie's role in household management was discussed, two important points came out. First, Charlie had an investment in being a "real man," and for him this meant that the father's role was to dominate the family and "rule it with an iron fist." Second, Charlie thought that this idea of the father's role was completely natural and effective. As Maude gave Charlie new information about how that made her feel, Charlie began to change.

Maude and Charlie moved through their first round of recontracting nicely. They were still a long way from an entirely effective relationship, but several of the most

troublesome parts of the relationship had been dealt with.
The revised contract looked like this:

**Charlie
promised to**

: keep the lines
of communication
open, recontract
when necessary,
and help Maude
grow as a person.

: go out
into the world
and work
for a living.

: be faithful
to Maude.

: not discuss
Maude's weaknesses
and fears
in front of others,
and provide support
so that
she will grow
and become
self-reliant.

: provide
companionship
at certain times,
placing Maude's
needs before those
of hunting friends.

**In return
Charlie expects to**

: be able
to call upon Maude
as a partner
in growth.

: rest
when he comes home
and not be bothered
by "little things"
—except when
they are not little
to Maude.

: have the last word
on family decisions.

: not be questioned
about his job.

: negotiate
minor irritations.

: be sexually satisfied
when
he so desires.

: be valued
as a real,
unique person.

: go hunting
with the "boys"
for two days
each year.

: negotiate problems.

**Maude
promised to**

: keep the lines
of communication
open, recontract
when necessary,
and help Charlie
grow as a person.

: take care
of the house
and children.

: take care
of some
of Charlie's
physical needs.

: love, honor,
and cherish Charlie.

: provide
companionship
for Charlie.

: negotiate
about Charlie's
"ways."

**In return
Maude expects to**

: be able
to call upon Charlie
as a partner
in growth.

: have protection
from
the world,
but move
toward self-reliance.

: get companionship
from
Charlie.

: enjoy
relative
faithfulness
from
Charlie.

: relate to Charlie
as a person.

: negotiate problems.

As you can see, several major changes have been made in the contract. One of the most important was that both Charlie and Maude reaffirmed their love of and need for the other partner. Both of them needed to be told that they were OK once in a while. Both of them needed to become more aware of how their behavior affected the other.

The following exercises
are provided
to help you
take a look
at your own needs
and examine
ways that you relate
to others
through contracts.

CLARIFYING MY NEEDS

This exercise is designed to help you clarify your own needs and desires. Each person has a general idea of the good life. List ten things you want most out of life:

1

4

2

5

3

6

7

8

9

10

Place a *C*
beside each of the items
you chose
in the Adult ego state.

Place an *A*
beside each of the items
you have acted upon
in the last two weeks.

Would achieving
satisfaction of these needs
violate any contracts
you have with your friends
and associates?

CLARIFYING MY CONTRACTS

Many times people have contracts they
do not fully understand from an Adult
position. This exercise will help you
review your contracts and bring them
fully into your conscious Adult. Try the
exercise with one contract at a time.

 1

With whom
is this contract drawn?

 2

How was this contract made?
Was it talked about,
or did it just happen
over a period of time?

 3

List your obligations
under this contract.

4

List as many things
as possible
that you are obligated to *not* do
under this contract.

 5

Do you think
that this contract
is helpful to both parties?

 6

Are there
elements of the contract
you would like to change?

RECONTRACTING

Once you have clarified your own needs and have looked at the nature of your existing contracts, you may want to develop more effective contracts. The following points are helpful in this process.

 Set aside a special time when you will not be interrupted and can talk with your co-contractor for a while.

 Focus upon both your own growth needs and the growth needs of the person with whom you are recontracting. Focus upon the positive potential of the relationship. What can you both get from the relationship? (Avoid blaming and evaluating the other person.)

Most people who are involved
in recontracting have some
negative feelings
about the existing contract.
Examine your feelings
and the expectations
that the other person has for you.
Make sure that those feelings
are treated in the new contract.

 Attend to open communication.
Important areas of concern
must not be avoided.
Make sure that expectations
on both sides are clear.

 Set some time in the future
to reevaluate the new contract.

Dr. Phillips
and Dr. Cordell
hold workshops in several major cities.
If you would like to be on the mailing list
for workshop brochures,
send your name to:

OK-ness Workshops
Box 626
Greeley, Colorado 80631